D1561807

The Way of Love

*Also available from Marshall Pickering
by the same author*

HEAVEN ON EARTH
FORTY DAYS AND FORTY NIGHTS

The Way of Love

Following Christ through Lent to Easter

BROTHER RAMON SSF

Illustrated by Molly Dowell

Marshall Pickering
An Imprint of HarperCollinsPublishers

Marshall Pickering is an Imprint of
HarperCollins*Religious*
Part of HarperCollins*Publishers*
77–85 Fulham Palace Road, London W6 8JB

First published in Great Britain
in 1994 by Marshall Pickering

1   3   5   7   9   10   8   6   4   2

Text copyright © 1994 Brother Ramon SSF
Illustrations copyright © 1994 Molly Dowell
Cover photograph of the author by Molly Dowell

Brother Ramon and Molly Dowell assert the moral right to be
identified as the author and illustrator of this work

A catalogue record for this book is
available from the British Library

ISBN 0 551 02818-1

Printed and bound in Great Britain by
HarperCollinsManufacturing Glasgow

CONDITIONS OF SALE

This book is sold subject to the condition that it
shall not, by way of trade or otherwise, be lent, re-sold,
hired out or otherwise circulated without the publisher's
prior consent in any form of binding or cover other
than that in which it is published and without a
similar condition including this condition being
imposed on the subsequent purchaser.

All rights reserved. No part of this publication may be
reproduced, stored in a retrieval system, or transmitted,
in any form or by any means, electronic, mechanical,
photocopying, recording or otherwise, without the prior
permission of the publishers

In gratitude for care and fellowship, to
Brother Dominic Christopher SSF
Brother Amos SSF

Scripture quotations taken from the Holy Bible,
New International Version.
Copyright © 1973, 1978, 1984 by International Bible Society.
Used by permission of Hodder & Stoughton Ltd.
All rights reserved.

"NIV" is a registered trademark of International Bible Society.
UK trademark number 1448790.

Contents

INTRODUCTION

A Place for Prayer and Meditation

MAKING THE JOURNEY

You are invited to a sterner discipline than merely giving up sugar for Lent! It is the discipline of a pilgrimage, a journey into scripture, a journey into your deepest self, a journey into God. Like all good disciplines, positive good emerges with accompanying joy, and closer proximity to that union in Love which is the goal of all our journeyings. We are all on pilgrimage anyway – from the cradle to the grave, and through the gateway of death into eternity. So any smaller pilgrimages on this larger journey which can infuse meaning and joy into life's twisting and (hopefully) ascending pathway, should be treasured.

It is in the nature of life's journey to include days of spring sunshine where bounding life and vitality initiate the adventure, running into summer days of lingering on plateaux of shared work and play, sustained by the bread and wine of loving communion and spurred on by personal and corporate vision. The pathway becomes more difficult and yet more rewarding in the autumn mists of unknowing, with the fruitful contemplative vistas of mature understanding. Then there are the wintry blasts of icy wind and freezing fog which we have to suffer for ourselves or on behalf of our loved ones.

Yet the path does not decline into the valley of the shadow of death, but is meant to be gently ascending into the greater mystery and deeper awareness of the divine Love. It is a personal and a corporate journey, but whether alone or with others, we are called into the deeper fellowship of Christ our Saviour, Friend and Brother.

Indeed, the whole pilgrimage is centred upon him. He is our fellow pilgrim who accompanies us on the way, and dwells within us on the journey. We tread in the footsteps of the historical Jesus, and we commune in mystical vision with the indwelling Christ. It is the Holy Spirit who makes the Christ personal and real to us on this pilgrimage, and it is toward the glory of the Father that we move. The scriptures are our map and the sacraments sustain us on the way from earth to heaven.

USING THE BOOK

The discipline for this journey is modest, for it is a mistake to bite off more than you can chew! It asks for up to an hour each day of Lent, and if this book is used with a group, seven weekly meetings. You should try to set aside an hour at the same time every day and make it sacrosanct, for it is your trysting-time with God. If your responsibilities make this difficult, then set aside a shorter period of time that is manageable for you; only try to make it regular. All discipline brings a reward and you may well find yourself *wanting* to set more time aside as you draw nearer to Holy Week! A very good practice, if you have the room, is to make a worship place, a 'space for God' in some corner, consisting of a low table or shelf with a candle, an open Bible, perhaps an icon or cross, and some flowers, with a cushion or prayer-stool.

Spend a few minutes of quiet, centring yourself within the presence and love of God, perhaps repeating the *Jesus Prayer* or a verse like 'Breathe on me, Breath of God . . .' Then, when you feel relaxed, take up the day's scripture, going through it slowly, feeding upon it meditatively. Follow that with the reflection provided, referring back to the scripture, and gently lead on to the prayer. Then spend the rest of the time up to the hour in openness before God, perhaps taking up the suggested response into your prayers. End the session with the *Gloria Patri*,* and carry the theme into the day's work.

The layout of this book is simple if you anchor yourself at its beginning on the eve of Ash Wednesday.

SHARING IN A GROUP

Groups may meet on seven occasions, after each section of the study. It can be left to members of the group to bring to the meeting thoughts on their journey from any of the themes of the previous week, or particular members may be asked beforehand to prepare a few minutes on one of the days' readings.

These groups are not meant to be formal Bible study or discussion groups. They are rather 'sharing the fruit of meditation'. If a word, a verse, a thought, a passage has warmed your heart, then share the experience with the group. Let the others feel your doubts, glimpse your joys, accompany you on that part of your journey; and then listen to them, hold them, carry them in your heart, and be illumined by the fellowship. If there are more than twelve meeting in one place it may be well to divide into further groups, numbering between seven and twelve.

Don't be afraid of sharing your own thoughts on the text, or your own pilgrimage experiences, for they are *yours*, and no one can deny or gainsay them. Groups sometimes do contain people who like the sound of their own voice or opinions, and they can be verbose and pompous. The simple, humble, trembling sharing of your thoughts or experiences may well be the very word of God to those in the group in real need of a sign or touch from him, for 'Consider your own call, brothers and sisters: not many of you were wise by human standards, not many were powerful, not many were of noble birth. But God chose what is foolish in the world to shame the wise; God chose what is weak in the world to shame the strong; God chose what is low and despised in the world . . . so that no one might boast in the presence of God.' (1 Corinthians 1:26-29)

Scattered through the Response sections are suggestions for practical action. These can be taken up by the reader on a personal basis or may spark the group or parish into corporate action, and this may carry on well after Easter.

Take up the invitation of this Lent pilgrimage then, whether on a personal level or within the context of group meetings. In any case, it is meant to supplement, and not supplant, your wider fellowship within the Church.

This is an ecumenical book for any Christian believer whose feet are set on the pilgrimage of discipleship. You will find that if you share this lesser pilgrimage during the coming Lent, it will place your larger human journey in the context of eternity.

Brother Ramon SSF

Gloria Patri alternatives from *The Daily Office SSF*
Glory to the Father, and to the Son,
   and to the Holy Spirit:
as it was in the beginning, is now,
   and shall be for ever. Amen.

or

Glory to God, Source of all being,
   Eternal Word and Holy Spirit:
as it was in the beginning, is now,
   and shall be for ever. Amen.

BEGINNING
Jesus, Man for Everyone

Remember you are dust

Shrove Tuesday

No More Alleluias

MATTHEW 16:5–12; 1 CORINTHIANS 5:6–8

*T*hen they understood that [Jesus] had not told them to beware of the yeast of bread, but of the teaching of the Pharisees and Sadducees.

Let us celebrate the festival, not with the old yeast, the yeast of malice and evil, but with the unleavened bread of sincerity and truth.

In our Franciscan Office Book there is a liturgical note for Shrove Tuesday which says: 'After Night Prayer, "Alleluia" is not said again until Easter Day.' I used to think this very odd, and I always find it difficult, because between Shrove Tuesday and Easter Day, even though it is the penitential season of Lent, I am sometimes bowled over by the mercy and love of God, and spontaneously cry "Alleluia!" I mean, is there *really* a ban on singing

Alleluia! Alleluia! Give thanks to the risen Lord,
Alleluia! Alleluia! Give praise to his name.

Well, yes there is! But it is only a liturgical ban. I find this friendly proscription very useful, because holding my Alleluias in check constantly reminds me of the meaning of Lent. During these 'forty odd days' there are themes of penitence, sorrow, temptation, pain, suffering and violence, and these are all reflected in the sadness of our aching and wounded world.

With the dawning of Easter Day, the surge of life energizes life and worship, and one of the most beautiful experiences is, after the morning darkness and Paschal fire in the monastery, celebrating the resurrection of Jesus, for he is the Sun of Righteousness rising from the darkness of death as the created sun is rising in the east. Emerging from the Easter eucharist into the spring sunshine is liturgical celebration *par excellence*.

I am writing these words just after Shrove Tuesday, and this morning I woke in my hermitage to a freezing temperature. Yet the trees and shrubs in my enclosure are budding and putting forth tiny leaves, especially lilac, viburnum and alder. It is a kind of restrained suggestion of spring, for the real Alleluias will burst forth with my 200 daffodil bulbs on Easter Day.

Then there are the pancakes. I made and tossed (success-fully) sweet pancakes on Shrove Tuesday, even though I was not really clearing out the yeast and leaven. But I was observ-ing the symbolism. The ancient Israelites cleared out the leaven from their homes in their liturgical celebration of the Passover (Exodus 12:14–20). Their leaven was the influence of pagan Egypt when they left its corruption as pilgrims for the wilderness and the promised land.

So it became the 'leaven on influence' when Jesus warned

9

his disciples of the pervasive and corrupting influence of the teaching of the Pharisees and Sadducees of his day. Paul thought of the leavening influence of pride, malice and evil, contrasting it with the 'unleavened bread of sincerity and truth'.

You would have been amused to see me tossing my pancakes in the hut on Shrove Tuesday. As I did so, I asked the Lord to help me clear out the leavening influences of malice and hypocrisy in my own life (and religious sins are particularly insidious). Because 'Shrove' comes from the 'shriven' aspect of confession, I also confessed my sins and received absolution by the mercy of God.

So at the beginning of this Lenten journey I shall continue to restrain my Alleluias. But having 'made a good Lent', I shall burst forth in abundant praise of our dear and sorrowing Lord, rejoicing with him in his resurrection glory on Easter Day.

PRAYER

Christ Jesus, Lord of creation:
  How can I be silent when the world of nature is stirring
    from the icy bands of winter and beginning to move into
    spring?
  How can I restrain my Alleluias when I am moved to awe
    and wonder at the mercy which reaches me in my sins
    and sicknesses, and raises me gently by grace?
  Yet I shall be restrained and mindful of the sorrow and pain
    of Gethsemane and Calvary during this Lenten pilgrimage;

Enable me to make this journey sharing your sorrow and joy,
Lord Jesus, so that the light at the end of the tunnel will
cause me to cry, with renewed gladness: 'Alleluia'. Amen.

RESPONSE

Take a walk today, Shrove Tuesday, and let the mood of the
season speak to you of aspects of the Gospel which you will
consider during Lent.

It is freezing and ice-bound? Then reflect on the colder
winter of death, and the sorrow and pain which our Lord
faced for us in his temptation and suffering. Is it almost balmy
with the promise of spring? Then let the tiny buds and new
leaves strengthen your weariness after winter, and reflect
upon the promise of new life in spring.

Let the Holy Spirit minister to you on this walk, and apply
the teaching in your own life. After the mingled joys and
sorrows of your earthly Lenten pilgrimage you will enter into
the eternal spring of heaven, and the beginning of all things
new.

Groups

This Response can be arranged for a group exercise. Members
may meet together for the scripture and prayer above; then
go singly for the reflective walk, returning to share volun-
tarily; finally ending with a brief silence and prayer.

11

Ash Wednesday

Ashes of Mortality

JOEL 2:12–14; MATTHEW 16:21–26

*Return to me with all your heart, with fasting, with
weeping, and with mourning; rend your hearts and not
your clothing. Return to the Lord your God, for he is gracious
and merciful, slow to anger, and abounding in steadfast love.*

It was during the season of Lent that converts in the early
Church were prepared for Easter baptism. Also during this
time those penitents who had been separated by notorious
sins were reconciled by penitence and absolution. So
repentance, forgiveness, reconciliation and instruction ran
into Easter joy, and that is the purpose of our observance of
Lent. The way in which penitence can mingle with adoration
and worship is beautifully illustrated in Allegri's setting of the
Miserere (Psalm 51), which is sometimes broadcast by the BBC
during Evensong today.

It is also on this day that a very simple 'Imposition of
Ashes' takes place in some churches. I have always been
profoundly moved by it, for it is not only a token of
penitence, but a physical mark and reminder of our mortality,
as is made clear by this prayer over the ashes:

Almighty God, you have created us out of the dust of the earth:

Grant that these ashes may be to us a sign of our mortality and penitence, that we may remember that it is only for your gracious gift that we are given everlasting life; through Jesus Christ our Saviour. Amen.

Then the priest/minister's thumb is dipped into the ashes, and the penitent's forehead is crossed with the words: 'Remember that you are dust, and to dust you shall return.' I shall never forget quietly moving along the altar rail making the sign of the cross at St Mary's Cathedral, Glasgow, when one of the young mothers held up her tiny baby to receive the ash upon his forehead.

We cannot evade this dual message of penitence and mortality at the beginning of our Lenten pilgrimage. Peter, in our gospel reading, was recovering from an amazingly high moment of inspiration when he had confessed Jesus as Messiah. Then, suddenly, he was confronted with Jesus prophesying his suffering and death. Here was perplexity and amazement. 'God forbid it, Lord,' he said, 'This must never happen to you.' Even more perplexing, Jesus, who had attributed his earlier inspiration to God, now attributed this rebuke to the influence of Satan!

Peter learned the hard way, through pride, failure and confession. He had his own Lenten journey to undertake, but at the last followed his Lord through death into the glory that lay beyond the cross.

PRAYER

Jesus, Lord of the journey:
At the beginning of this pilgrimage the road must have
seemed full of pain and sorrow as you set your face
toward Jerusalem.
Without you as Saviour and elder brother I shall fall, fail
and go astray. Place your arm of encouragement around
my drooping shoulder, Lord; lift up my head that I may
see the glory shining at the end of the valley; help me
take the first determined steps of faith. Amen.

RESPONSE

Either go with your group to share in the Ash Wednesday
liturgy this evening, or pre-record the BBC Ash Wednesday
Evensong and let the group listen prayerfully with a lighted
candle in their midst.

Thursday after Ash Wednesday

Tempted by the Devil

MATTHEW 4:1–11

Jesus said to him, 'Away with you, Satan! For it is written: "Worship the Lord your God, and serve only him."' Then the devil left him, and suddenly angels came and waited on him.

This was not the only experience of temptation by Satan, but it was the basic one, the definitive one, the one which confirmed Jesus' purpose once and for all towards light, life and love. Once this battle was won the work of redemption was well under way. The temptations were real, they were not shadow-boxing or play-acting, but it was also true that the Holy Spirit had set the context, and it becomes clear that Satan's malice was turned into Jesus' victory.

There are demonic forces unleashed in our world. They may be encountered in the secret places of the human soul, suddenly confronting the man or woman unexpectedly with such horror and vileness that the human heart is shocked that it is capable of such evil. Or they may be encountered as psychic forces which are larger than any one person, concentrated in corporate commercial or financial projects. These may traffic in arms, manufacture instruments of torture for political use, gas or germ warfare, or profit from drug and chemical addictions on a massive scale. They may empower the military might of nations in technological warfare, the end justifying the means until many millions of innocent people are tortured and killed on every side. There may be dark angels behind world dictators. All the while, the cosmic and personal power of Satan is hidden, and made to look like something else.

Jesus recognized all this as he was caught up in the temptations which mingled physical need, loneliness, a struggle with his vocation, and the subtle offers of personal, corporate and political power to achieve what seemed to be ultimate good. Polluted rivers can only lead to a contaminated ocean, and so the subtle means of manipulation and magic can only lead to the rule of violence and oppression. Jesus, after the ecstasy of his baptism, saw into the depths of his own heart, became aware of the various offered techniques of bringing in the kingdom. He recognized the dark seduction of worldly power which corrupts the way of suffering love.

But what about you and me as we begin this pilgrimage of Lent? We are not largely responsible for people and nations; we have no vocation to a messianic role; we are not called to redeem the world. We have to translate the temptations of Jesus to see what they mean to us. Perhaps they mean something like this:

Stones into bread. My temptation is gluttony – spending inordinate amounts on connoisseur food and frequently eating out, regardless of cost. My temptation is lust – feeding my sexual fantasies with soft porno magazines, secretly watching violent and sadistic sexual videos, and finding sexual encounters away from home.

16

Throw yourself down. My temptation is showmanship. I court favour, project a favourable image, make friends in order to influence people, flaunt my charismatic personality; make out that I'm more loving, compassionate, discerning, understanding and sympathetic than I really am – and all for self-aggrandizement and human praise.

Offer of power. My temptation is manipulation of others. As a husband or wife I want to 'mould' my partner, make the major decisions. As a parent I require obedience without question. At work I play one colleague off against another for personal gain. In a group I want to have everyone's attention and if they don't agree with me I blame them for not listening properly.

When people as described above succumb to such temptations it is bad enough for their own life, but worse for the family. In a position of influence in society the repercussions multiply, and they can be a source of evil – the instrument of the devil.

Jesus resisted the subtle doubts and evil suggestions from the powers of darkness. He offered himself wholly to God in personal humility, took the path of simplicity and put no trust in shows of charismatic power or political manoeuvring. He was able to withstand the crushing temptation and desolation of Gethsemane and Calvary because he had set his face towards the will of God here, in the wilderness.

PRAYER

Lord Jesus, strengthener of the tempted:
You spent forty days and nights of privation, suffering and
temptation in the wilderness, discerning the web of lies
and deceit which Satan presented to you as the path you
should tread.
Grant me such discernment, Lord, when I am surrounded by
the world, the flesh and the devil, and in your strength
let me overcome. Amen.

RESPONSE

Have you honestly and with integrity faced yourself in the solitude of your own desert? Have you shared those areas of duplicity and hypocrisy that you suspect have deep roots in your soul, with a brother or sister you can trust? Perhaps this is the time to look for such a person, for 'soul-friend sharing' can lead to profound mutual trust with a fellow pilgrim on the way.

Groups
In the context of today's theme, share your thoughts about the value of a soul-friend/spiritual director.

Friday after
Ash Wednesday

Fasting and Sharing

ISAIAH 58:1-9; MATTHEW 6:16-18

Is this not the fast that I choose: to loose the bonds of injustice . . . to let the oppressed go free, and to break every yoke? Is it not to share your bread with the hungry, and bring the homeless poor into your house?

Voluntary fasting is a luxury in a world in which most of the people are hungry and many are dying of starvation. So when a well-fed and cosseted congregation indulges in token fasts and rituals it deserves to be castigated by the prophet and chastised by a just and compassionate God. 'I hate, I despise your festivals, I take no delight in your solemn assemblies . . .' cries God against his people who fast and cry and weep and chant, who burn incense and bow and pray and engage in ritual (Amos 5:21-24). What God really demands is compassion and justice, practical self-sacrifice in order that the poor might profit. The compassion of the prophets is real but not sentimental. The love of God is disciplined and firm. Indeed the anger of God is an aspect of his love. It is not the bad temper of a tyrant, but the burning discipline of a loving father who acts for the good of his children.

So this Lent, any symbolic or ritualistic liturgy is good *if* it

19

leads to purity of heart and openness of hand to the poor and the needy. No amount of religious practice, catholic or charismatic, is a scrap of use unless it produces compassion, which, in turn, leads to practical help. You may take this book, and set aside an hour a day right through Lent in diligent study and saying prayers. But if your heart is not purified and set on the love of God, you may as well not have bothered.

These days of Lent, especially as we enter Holy Week, are filled with symbolic observances which demonstrate and portray the Gospel with liturgical beauty and meaning. As a means of grace they point towards Christ, the centre, in and for whom our worship is offered.

The Fridays of Lent, for instance, may be used as fast days. You can go without solid food for one or all meals as a mark of penitence, to sharpen your prayer life, and to identify with the hungry. But then take the money which would have been spent on food and channel it to the relief of someone's suffering. In that way your liturgical observance will serve the purposes of true piety and compassion. And that is the kind of religion which is acceptable to God (James 1:27).

Such observances, when used and valued aright, channel our love and prayers into works of mercy which actually accomplish something. The sick are cared for, the prisoners visited, the hungry fed, the naked clothed, the lonely comforted, the homeless housed. There are also social and political implications to all this, of course, but today let it begin in *your* heart − and now.

PRAYER

Searching and sympathizing Saviour:
You gaze into the deep places of the heart and search out
the hidden motives;
Forgive me for my duplicity and hypocrisy, even using
religion to prop up my own piety and as a display before
others;
Grant that my love for God and for my neighbour may not
degenerate into mere sentiment, but that it may be
disciplined and channelled into practical help for my
fellows. Amen.

RESPONSE

Either use this Friday in Lent as a family fast, collecting the
resulting money to use for an anonymous gift for a neighbour,
or as a group, fast channelling the money to Tear Fund,
Cafod, etc.

Saturday after Ash Wednesday

The Joy of Repentance

JOHN 4:4-30

The woman left her water jar and went back to the city. She said to the people, 'Come and see a man who told me everything I have ever done! He cannot be the Messiah, can he?' They left the city and were on their way to him.

One of the choruses I learned as a child ran:

Jesus gave her water that was not in the well;
She went away singing, she came back bringing
Others to the water that was not in the well.

That's what the story is about. Not only had the woman misunderstood Jesus' offer of living water, but she had been using religious controversy (Jewish versus Samaritan theology) as a shield against God, and had messed up the meaning of life and love in her own personal relationships.

There was a great deal of untangling to do: personal, moral, religious, theological. It seemed formidable, but really became very simple because Jesus went to the heart of her need, and she was willing to let her soul be exposed to him. She became one of those people who opens up to God as a bud opens to the radiance of the sun.

She could have hidden behind the bitter enmity which had raged between Jews and Samaritans from the time of Ezra and Nehemiah, or between the rival claims of Mount Zion and Mount Gerazim. She need not have been so honest about her moral life. But she allowed the vulnerable and tired Jesus to lead her out of her own weariness and pseudo-religion into gazing upon the face of the Messiah. And that look swept away all her sins and fears, bringing her repentance and joy. If she had known the hymn, she could have sung:

O Saviour Christ, You too are man,
You have been troubled, tempted, tried;
Your kind but searching glance can scan
The very wounds that shame would hide.

He looked upon her searchingly, and that saving look brought forgiveness and joy. That is the way that we shall learn repentance during this Lent. All the sorrow and pain of the Via Dolorosa, the Way of Sorrows, will lead us to the hill called Calvary, to the rocky tomb in the garden, and to a confrontation with the crucified and risen Jesus. The second stanza of that childhood chorus ran:

Jesus still gives water that is not in the well;
You'll go away singing, and come back bringing
Others to the water that is not in the well.

23

PRAYER

Lord Jesus, Saviour and Friend:
The woman came wearily with her water jar to Jacob's well
in the heat of the day. There she met your searching eyes,
probing the depths of her soul. And there she trembled
with awe and the joy of penitence, leading to forgiveness
and peace.
Search me today, Lord, and bring me to sorrow for my sins
and my misunderstanding of love. Under the scrutiny of
your searching but loving eyes, expose the hidden secrets
of my heart, and lead me at last to forgiveness and joy.
Amen.

RESPONSE

Is your life shabby? Have you become entangled in domin-
ating or unsavoury relationships? Do you use your religion as
a shield against the reality of God?

Christ searches the depths of your life today, and longs for
you to leave the old water jar of what used to be, to drink
of the new and living water that he offers with the accompanying transformation of your whole life. Stay with the
story, open your heart to God in prayer and let him show
you yourself, and the way in which transformation can begin.

Perhaps you should go to a trusted priest, minister or
fellow Christian and make a complete and open confession of
all the sins and secrets, the hopes and longing in your heart.
It may be right to write out such a confession so that it may

be laid before God and, as the words of forgiveness are said by the brother/sister, the confession can be burned. And your repentance will lead to joy.

LENT 1
Jesus, Man of Stories

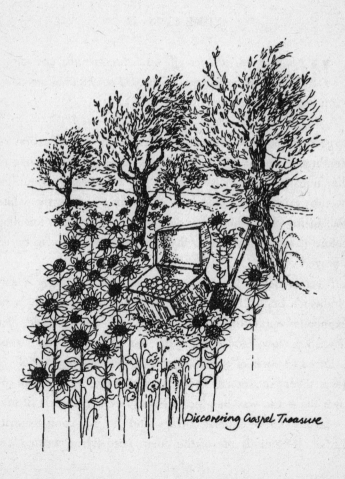

Discovering Gospel Treasure

Lent 1: Sunday

Enfolded in Love

LUKE 15:11–32

While he was still far off, his father saw him and was filled with compassion; he ran and put his arms around him and kissed him.

I recently mounted on wood a very large reproduction of Rembrandt's painting *The Return of the Prodigal Son* for one of the nuns at Tymawr convent. It was huge, beautiful, overpowering; and while it stood waiting against the white wall in my chapel hut I was almost brought to tears kneeling before it to say my offices. It seemed to tower above me as I prayed.

I remembered how moved I was when reading Henri Nouwen's book, *The Return of the Prodigal Son* in which he expounds upon this beautiful painting and parable. He described how God dealt with him, showing him to be pictured in each of the characters in this amazing parable of Jesus. Every movement in the story stirs up the depths of my own life – the way in which I have grieved the heart of love – in my fellow human beings and in my compassionate Father. It reminds me of the poem Lord Byron wrote, 'On

This Day I Complete my Thirty-Sixth Year', a stanza of which reads:

> *My days are in the yellow leaf,*
> *The flowers and fruits of love are gone;*
> *The worm, the canker and the grief*
> *Are mine alone.*

The Prodigal Son begged for penance and penalty, but the father knew he had drained the dregs of shame, helplessness, frustration and sorrow. The boy hoped for mercy, but was overwhelmed by love. The father was not testing him by waiting. He waited because he would not, could not, force his love. The father waited, yearned, wept, gazed along the road – and as soon as he saw his son 'still far off' his compassion burst into flame, and he ran, ran along the road. The Greek text says *kataphileo* – he kissed him tenderly, endearingly, affectionately. The narrative is alive with excitement, and portrays the old man seeing, pitying, running, falling, kissing and embracing his dear, penitent son.

The boy is overwhelmed and stumbles over his confession, pouring out his sorrow, pleading forgiveness. As I look at Rembrandt's beautiful painting and see the bedraggled, dirty, weary, helpless son, on his knees with his head buried in the bosom of the embracing father, I can hear him say, 'My son, my son . . . I don't care where you've been, what you've done, how far you've wandered – today you're home, you're in my arms, and you're mine!' Mother Julian understands:

In his love he clothes us,
Enfolds and embraces us;
That tender love completely surrounds us,
Never to leave us.

Is God *really* like that? He didn't tell the boy to work off his debt in a year's hard labour – from pigsty to cattle pen. But he kissed him, embraced him, garlanded him with a robe, a ring, and sandals of freedom.

Yes, God is *really* like that! That's why I found myself going for a gentle jog in the cold, winter darkness before dawn a few days ago, through the fields, and down the monastery track. On my way back I began to sing and dance in the field before the Lord. As I danced, the bell began to ring in the monastery for morning prayer and eucharist, and I returned to my hermitage hut, warmed with the love of God.

PRAYER

My compassionate Father:
I tremble before the immensity of your love, for you not
only forgive my sins, but restore me to your heart. You
invade my soul with joy, you wash me with your tears
and embrace me with compassion.
Oh, what will it be when I come to the gates of glory? And
what will it be to be received into the eternal love when
this pilgrimage on earth is over, and I come home at last?
Enfold me in your love, now and for ever. Amen.

RESPONSE

Open your Bible at this parable and read it slowly (if possible with a reproduction of Rembrandt's painting). Have you a father's, a mother's heart? Reflect on your own parents – do you need their forgiveness? Have you forgiven them if there is need? Do you have children (physical or spiritual)? What about them?

Let God hold you to his heart. Don't be afraid to weep, to sing, to be silent. If your parents/children are around, visit or write them, and let God melt all your coldness.

Groups
Let one member read the parable and the Response above by candlelight, followed by fifteen minutes of silence.

Lent 1: Monday

My Neighbour is Humankind

LUKE 10:25–37

'*Which of these three, do you think, was a neighbour to the man who fell into the hands of the robbers?*' he said.

'*The one who showed him mercy.*'

Jesus said to him, 'Go and do likewise.'

Jerusalem is 2,300 feet above sea level. Jericho is 1,300 feet below sea level, so the road descends sharply and is nearly twenty miles long, through deserted country. Jerome, in the fourth century, said that it was still infested with Bedouin robbers, and it is still the same today.

The lawyer in the reading asked Jesus a theological question, and received an answer that probed the man's theology and practice, for these two cannot be separated. The 'answer' to the question of eternal life is to love God utterly, with the whole of one's being, and flowing from that is the love of one's neighbour. Where love is poured in, then love will flow. But the lawyer wanted to know *who* is neighbour, and *how* it could be done. So Jesus told the story – and the story brought the man to see the amazing love of God, to feel the bankruptcy of false religion, to perceive the radiance of God wherever love is manifested, and to realize that the love of God is found in the unlikeliest places, among the unlikeliest people. My neighbour is the woman, the man, the child, close at hand – whatever colour of face, whatever creed professed, whatever state that one is in – if they are human, then they are neighbour, and worthy to be loved.

This is an amazing story, for Jews and Samaritans were bitterest enemies who would not even speak to each other. And it is here that Jesus finds human compassion. I would not pretend that I am not religious, and I presume that you, the reader, are too. But what *kind* of religion? It is better to have none at all than a religion which is heartless, legalistic, fanatical, exclusive. The priest may have been hurrying to a committee meeting for the cleaning up of the Jericho road. The Levite may have avoided ritual contamination by touching a corpse. Religious reasons for passing him by!

What can this story mean for me? Well at least these things:

1. I should see the image and love of God in every needy person. If I say I love God and hate my brother and sister, I'm a liar (1 John 4:20), and no amount of religious claptrap or ritual will get me into heaven, for God hates that kind of religion (Amos 5:21-24).
2. Then I should *be aware* of human need, *feel* compassion, and *act* in mercy. My believing, my feeling and my doing should move in harmony. Faith is basic, but if compassion does not flow from it then it is pseudo-faith and I am deluding myself, though I cannot deceive God.
3. I should not substitute talk, committees, liturgies or

ritual for the basic, simple, helping hand to those nearest me.

4. My heart should be open to a world-wide vision, to my brothers and sisters in all the world, for if I am human, nothing that is human should be alien to me.

I have been brought up on this story, and its basic teaching is clear. But I've also seen shades and levels of meaning which point to the divine Love. I cannot read the words 'he came to where the man was' (v 33 NIV) without thinking of the humble *kenosis* or self-emptying of Jesus in relinquishing the riches of glory for the poverty of our human lot to make us rich with his healing love (2 Corinthians 8:9). I don't want to make an allegory of this story as Augustine did, but my heart is moved by the way in which the Good Samaritan portrays the grace and compassion of my Saviour Jesus. The old hymn says it:

> *He found me bruised and dying,*
> *And poured in oil and wine;*
> *He whispered to assure me:*
> *'I've found you, you are mine.'*
> *I never heard a sweeter voice,*
> *It made my aching heart rejoice.*

> *O the love that sought me,*
> *O the blood that bought me,*
> *O the grace that brought me to the fold*
> *Wondrous grace that brought me to the fold.*

I see, therefore, that this is an evangelical story of the poor sinner, sick and wounded with sin, robbed of his innocence and left for dead. It is the story of a Saviour who came in compassion, pouring in the wine of cleansing, the oil of healing, the grace of restoration.

It is also a social and political story of living in openness and compassion to every other human being – indeed every sentient being (donkey included!). It teaches personal and corporate works of mercy, the alleviation of human suffering, and the provision of basic, human needs for my neighbour.

But it is also a story of eternal life, for that was the initial question. It is the story of a Saviour who will return again to ensure the full redemption of the victim and the restoration of the image of God in a new humanity. 'Which was the neighbour?' asked Jesus. 'The one who showed mercy,' replied the lawyer. And the divine response was: 'Go and do likewise.'

PRAYER

Jesus, Saviour of humankind:
You have taught us to seek out the lost and the lonely, the sick and the oppressed, the unwanted and the dying, and to minister to them in your name.
We are able to respond to such teaching because you have come to where we are, taking on our burdens and pains, pouring in the wine and oil of your compassion and healing.
Continue your sustaining care of our souls, that we in turn may stretch out a healing hand to our neighbours. Amen.

RESPONSE

Seek out (sensitively!) in your neighbourhood those unlikely neighbours you have neglected. Reach out in friendship and sharing to a family of a different religion, colour or creed — with no strings! If friendship develops, let it be a dialogue of mutual learning, sharing and help. Let there be repentance for past neglect, humility in present concern, and with hope for a fostering of neighbourliness.

Groups

Why not go as a group to a 'neighbouring' church service, or arrange a visit to a mosque, temple, synagogue or ashram? They may like to return the visit!

Lent 1: Tuesday
The Thrill of Discovery

MATTHEW 13:44–46

. . . treasure hidden in a field . . . in his joy he goes and sells all that he has and buys that field. Finding one pearl of great value, he went and sold all that he had and bought it.

I've always found this pair of parables attractive and exciting, and have always loved preaching on them. There is the romance and quest of hidden treasure and the breathtaking wonder of imagining the superlative pearl. These stories portray something of the Gospel as an adventurous and precious quality of life, rather than a drab and yawning set of legalistic rules.

First the treasure hidden in a field. Nothing led up to this discovery – it was sudden, unexpected, challenging, life-changing. It demanded immediate and critical action – surrendering everything else to possess the treasure. This is a sudden conversion story – like Saul on the road to Damascus, Augustine in the garden in Milan, Luther overwhelmed by the demand of faith, Wesley when his heart was strangely warmed. In a moment, everything is new! 'If anyone is in Christ, there is a new creation; everything old has passed away; see, everything has become new.' (2 Corinthians 5:17)

The remarkable discovery causes the labourer to sell everything to buy the field and possess the treasure. There is no sacrifice involved, for the sight of the treasure blinds the man to all else. When David Livingstone was reminded of the tremendous self-sacrifice he made in giving his life to Africa as a missionary, he said, 'I have never made a sacrifice in my life.' Everything else was irrelevant in the light of the treasure – the call of Christ. 'When a woman is in labour, she has pain, because her hour has come,' said Jesus. 'But when her child is born she no longer remembers the anguish because of the joy of having brought a human being into the world.' (John 16:21)

When the Gospel treasure of forgiveness, life, joy and peace are clearly seen in the Saviour Jesus, then all else can be flung away to possess this treasure, for everything else shrinks to nothing in comparison.

Then the priceless pearl. This discovery is not sudden, unexpected, or completely surprising. The merchant is a connoisseur of pearls. His search has taken him many years of travel, from the Persian Gulf to India. Then one day in the marketplace, in the hands of a trader who seems not to know its immense value, shines this pearl of a value beyond dreams. Nothing must stand in the way. He sells everything he has, including his whole collection of pearls gathered over many diligent years – simply for the joy of possessing *this* pearl. I love the hymn by John Mason, especially to the tune 'Lydia':

I've found the pearl of greatest price,
My heart, it sings for joy;
And sing I must, for Christ is mine,
Christ shall my song employ.

If the treasure hidden in a field represents Saul's sudden conversion on the Damascus road, then this pearl story illustrates his conviction after many years of diligent pursuit of a deeper life: 'For his sake I have suffered the loss of all things, and I regard them as rubbish, in order that I may gain Christ and be found in him.' (Philippians 3:8-9)

I remember once preaching on these parables and saying to the congregation, 'Have you been labouring away over many years, searching in quest of a life in which there is joy, love and peace, but feeling it has eluded you? Well, you've come to the right place today, you've landed in the right field, so take your spade in your hand and dig with me, and together we shall find hidden treasure – the joy and peace that is Christ himself.' There is a specific and uplifting joy in expository preaching that really engages preacher and congregation 'digging together'. The resulting unearthing of Gospel treasure is a shared communion of overflowing excitement. I have other joys now in my hermitage, but I do miss that relationship of digging, searching, discovering together, which is the specific joy of preaching the Word.

PRAYER

Dear and precious Lord:

There are times when we are occupied in our daily, wearying
tasks, not expecting to stumble upon hidden treasure; there
are times when we are tired with our searching, longing,
yearning for forgiveness, for healing, for peace;

Then you confront us with your loving presence, you offer us
relief from our burdens, peace for our anxieties, healing
for our sickness, and the treasure of your love.

When such moments come, let us recognize them, embrace
them, surrender all else, so that you may reign in the
inmost shrine of our hearts — for then we shall possess
that pearl of greatest price. Amen.

RESPONSE

Look among the 'possessions' of your relationships, material
goods, ambitions, and ask if any of them are keeping you
from the supreme treasure of compassionate love that Christ
offers. In order to live in such radical openness and love you
may be challenged to surrender some of your dearest plans,
or change the basic pattern of your life. Are you willing? Are
you ready? Are you even open to the possibility? You will not
be coerced, for love does not force its will — but what a loss
if you turn away.

Groups

Ask the above questions among yourselves regarding your
church life and your corporate responsibility as disciples of
Christ in your neighbourhood.

What is the great treasure, the pearl of great price in terms of a just and compassionate society? And what is it worth surrendering to obtain it? Is your church/fellowship prepared to search deeply, to be confronted with sacrifice? Are you?

Lent 1: Wednesday

Forgive as You are Forgiven

MATTHEW 18:23–35

Be merciful, just as your Father is merciful.

Peter asked Jesus how many times he should forgive someone
who injured him, and Jesus told the parable of the Unforgiving Debtor as a reply. I wonder what bad experience
Peter may have had? Or was it that he noticed Jesus reaching
out in understanding and compassion, and therefore wanted
to know if this was merely a duty, or evidence of something
far deeper in the life of the Spirit?

The basic story is that the king's official had borrowed (or
fiddled) upwards of a million pounds, and his sentence was
that he, his family and possessions should be sold. The man
threw himself down before the king and pleaded for time.
The king knew that the man could never pay, and in pity and
generosity forgave him without reserve. Soon afterwards,
meeting a fellow servant who owed him a paltry £5 the
former debtor took him by the throat in anger, crying, 'Pay
what you owe!' The second debtor fell down and pleaded as
the first had done. But this time there was no mercy. He was
flung into prison without pity. His friends went to the king
in distress and related what had happened, and the king

became angry and rewarded the unforgiving debtor with the same treatment as he had meted out to his fellow servant.

This does not answer the 'how many times' question that Peter asked, but points out the first principle of the grace of God — forgiveness that melts a sinner's heart and enables him or her to forgive in like manner. God's forgiveness is a fountain of grace, and is the basis for reconciliation and mutual love. The forgiven sinner cannot help but forgive. This story shows that our sins against the holy and loving God are like the enormous debt that the first servant owed, and that people who sin against us bear a paltry comparison. If God can, and does, forgive us freely and compassionately, then we sinners can only do the same, and therefore live in that state of forgiving love that transforms our lives on earth and radiates the same grace by which we have been forgiven.

We cannot forgive others before we are forgiven and reconciled, but when we are within the forgiven and forgiving family of God, then we are to forgive as we have been forgiven. If this principle does not have free play among us, then we have seriously to question whether we have truly received the divine forgiveness that melts the heart. It is not that God withholds his forgiveness, but that we erect barriers, close doors, harden our hearts, so that we are not capable of receiving, and therefore of offering to others, true forgiveness. We may allow envy, jealousy, malice to smoulder in our hearts. We may secretly rejoice at another's misfortune or withhold forgiveness from anyone who has spoken or acted against us, injuring our pride. God does not refuse to forgive us as a result, but he does say, 'I offer you forgiveness and grace, but you cannot receive it unless and until you have a loving and forgiving heart.'

It is clear that we cannot deal with God in one compartment of our lives, and with our fellows in another. A marriage can only grow as mutual forgiveness is shared. A friendship can only mature if differences and divergent views and temperaments are acknowledged, appreciated and allowed for. Otherwise estrangement takes place, turning to alienation, with a loss of spontaneity and peace. If we do not forgive, then we cannot be forgiven. If we are not compassionate, then we shall lose the spirit of compassion. If we are covetous, materialistic and legalistic in our relationships, then our souls will shrivel, and we shall lose the dimension of eternity.

This does not only hold in personal and family situations, but in the fellowship of the Church, in the workplace, in wider society between nations. Today, you can either initiate a brass chain of unforgiving hardness of heart which will be joined link by link until it imprisons those who have forged it, or you can initiate a golden chain of compassion and forgiveness which will link together fellow human beings in the dance of love.

PRAYER

Forgiving God and Saviour:
I have broken your laws and grieved your loving heart, but
    you have surrounded me with the forgiving love of your
    compassion.

Melt my heart in forgiving love towards others, I pray, that I may forgive as I have been forgiven, and so keep open that divine channel of mutual love which is at the heart of the Gospel of your saving grace. Amen.

RESPONSE

Do I bear a grudge, withhold forgiveness, or even perpetrate malice against another human being? Do I nurse a grievance, smoulder an offence, or allow the roots of bitterness to reach deep into my soul from an old injury against me?

Do I realize that I cannot initiate grace or forgiveness, but if I look to the fountainhead of God's grace, I will be enabled not only to be a *forgiven* sinner, but a *forgiving* sinner to all around?

Groups

Consider how church differences and antagonisms can cause schism in a local fellowship, and how denominational and communal differences have caused mutual antagonisms and excommunications in the history of the Church. How can such differences and schisms be healed? Share possibilities of new approaches to Christian unity in the Body of Christ.

Lent 1: Thursday

Eat, Drink and be Merry

LUKE 12:13–31

I will pull down my barns and build larger ones, and there
*I will say to my soul, 'Soul, you have ample goods laid up
for many years; relax, eat, drink, and be merry.' But God said
to him, 'You fool! This very night your life is being demanded
of you.'*

The wealthy farmer in this story was physically frenetically
active – pulling down and rebuilding; but spiritually over-
indulgent – 'relax, eat, drink, and be merry'. He saw no end
to his expanding schemes and upwardly mobile lifestyle, with
profits rolling in, unaffected by any recession. He seemed to
have no worries about sickness and mortality, and was one of
those we call the 'fat cats' of the world.

Do you remember the prominent life assurance company
which used to run illustrated press adverts showing a man
in four decades of his life? At twenty five, jauntily: 'They
say there's no pension with this job'; At thirty five, concerned: 'I wish there was a pension with this job'; At forty
five, anxious: 'I'm really worried that there's no pension with
this job'; At fifty five, desperate: 'I don't know what I'm
going to do without a pension.' These days neither jobs nor

pensions are safe with financial sharks in our commercial waters. But our man's worries were not about pensions, but about how he was going to cope with his snowballing profits. To his question, 'What shall I do?', it could be answered, 'Re-distribute to the poor', but such an answer would have fallen on deaf ears.

In our contemporary marketplace economy, finance dictates our every move — from the water we drink to super-expensive geriatric care and funerals which are an increasing source of worry to elderly people for years before they die. The accountant looms behind health, education and basic needs of warmth and shelter. The increasingly sad (but not new) scandal is the chasm between those who earn astronomical salaries and those who sleep in the streets and are ineligible for even basic survival allowance.

A little while ago, as a visiting friar, I concluded a sermon to a church congregation which got me some peculiar looks when I said, 'I know many of you haven't two pennies to rub together — but there are some of you who would not miss a thousand pounds or two from your bank balance. I'll tell you what I'd like you to do this week — send £100 to some needy family in your area. Don't think too long about it, just do it!' I wonder if any of them did?

The strange thing is that we always want a bit more. It was Seneca, I believe, who said, 'Money is like sea water — the more you drink, the thirstier you become.' My mother had a good answer to such an attitude: 'There are no pockets in shrouds!' This is what Jesus said about the rich fool.

This story is not simply an evangelical gospel parable which, like the one in Luke 16:19-31, says that if you are completely self-centred and indulgent in this life you will suffer in the next. No. This parable confronts the reader with the simple fact of mortality. Tonight your soul will be demanded. Then who will take over your possessions? To illustrate further, a wealthy atheist farmer boasted one day to his poor neighbour, 'Look north,' he pointed, 'all that you see is mine. Look south, all that you see is mine. Look east, all that you see is mine. Look west, all that you see is mine.' The poor farmer was silent for a moment, and then he pointed upwards and asked, 'How much do you own in that direction?'

The Gospel is not a negative set of 'don'ts'. Neither is it a teaching majoring on asceticism or mortification as a way of life. Jesus' offer was of life in all its fullness, and if he preached self-sacrifice (which he did) it was to cast off the second-best in order to achieve the best; a letting-go of the superfluous, hindering obstacles that cheat and deceive us, in order that we might enter into a simpler, happier, more open and loving way of existing. Nevertheless, there is a call to strip down excesses. It is a call to spiritual health, or even spiritual athleticism. In order to gain mastery, or win the prize, there is the discipline, the asceticism of surrendering the superfluous – for your own sake and the sake of others.

I know it is easy for the poor person to preach to the wealthy about redistribution of wealth, and one suspects that the same man or woman would cling to privileges of wealth and power if roles were reversed. We can test how far our market economy has taken us from Gospel values when I suggest that *you* should sell all your possessions and redistribute the money to the poor. Such words may sound sacrilegious, for money and productivity are the god Mammon set up in the marketplace, worshipped especially in the money strata of our society. I am not preaching Gospel communism to everyone, but what if it were required of *you*? It is probably not the case, but what if it were true that 'this very night your life is demanded of you'?

PRAYER

Lord Jesus, man of simplicity and integrity:
You were born in poverty and lived in simplicity; you worked
  with your hands and shared everything you possessed.
I am relatively poor in comparison with the wealthy of the
  world — let me always be grateful that I have not been
  tempted by great wealth and luxury;
I am relatively rich in comparison with most people of the
  world — let me share not only my abundance, but give
  sacrificially for the alleviation of the world's ills, and so
  follow in the pattern of your footsteps. Amen.

RESPONSE

What about those poor friends or neighbours? Even the sacrifice of a night out might pay their fuel bill. And why leave money when you die for relations to argue over? Give it away now — and see what joy it brings.

Groups

Has your church, locally or denominationally, got money stashed away or 'invested for profit'? Why not ask pertinent questions, start a ginger group for off-loading money? Why not put the poor, the missionary society, before organs, spires and fabric? What are your priorities?

Lent 1: Friday

Secure Foundations

LUKE 6:46–49

A man building a house dug deeply and laid the foundations on rock; when a flood arose, the river burst against that house but could not shake it, because it had been well built.

I'm faced with two contrasting structures. My hermitage is a simple wooden hut. Its foundations? Well it has none, for it was erected on two dozen breeze blocks! The second structure faces me – the stout, thirteenth-century red stone tower of Astley Church, rising from the woodlands about two miles away.

We've experienced pouring and incessant rain during the last months. The December and January winds have howled around me, and the rain has beaten against the hut and poured through the vegetable garden and my enclosure, down into the fields before me. But I'm still here. I happen to be in a fortunate spot – too high for floods and protected enough not to be too vulnerable. But I must not presume, for I had a letter this winter telling me of a fellow hermit in North Wales, where a chicken shed without foundations (plus the chickens) had taken off in the winter gales and has not been seen since.

I'm rather laid back about the safety of my hut, but I

wouldn't dream of taking such a risk with my immortal soul!
I am not building on sand (or breeze blocks) there, for the
foundation is driven into solid rock. As the old hymn says:

> On Christ the solid rock I stand,
> All other ground is sinking sand.

I am confident, but this is no presumption, no cocksure
affirmation of my own making. It is the assurance which is
grounded on Christ, confirmed in the Word of God and the
interior witness of the Holy Spirit in my heart. On the day
of judgement I cannot afford to have erected the superstructure of my life on some sort of good morality, sincere
humanism or popular religion. None of those things will stand
against the howling storms of finitude and mortality which
ultimately undermine every human life.

Wandering through a cemetery some time ago I came
across two contrasting inscriptions. The first said: 'He died as
he lived – a sportsman.' I don't think I'd want to stake my
eternal welfare on so flimsy a foundation. But the second was
of a thirty-three-year-old woman named Laura West. It ran:

> Happy Christian, God's own child,
> Chosen, called, and reconciled;
> Once a rebel far from God,
> Now brought near through Jesus' blood.

I believe she built upon the rock.

PRAYER

Great Master Builder:
When the storms of life engulf my soul, and I am surrounded
by the floods of tribulation, sickness and death, help me
to feel the security of the firm foundation which is Christ;
Assure me that though I may tremble on the rock, I cannot
be cast off or swept away, for my security is in your love,
your promises, and your redemption. Amen.

RESPONSE

As you make your way around today, note building structures
and their foundations, especially if new construction is taking
place in your neighbourhood. Then carry your observations
for sharing with your group, and ask two questions. First: 'Is
the foundation of my life rooted firmly in Christ?' Second:
'What is the quality of the superstructure erected on that
foundation?'

Lent 1: Saturday

Come, for Everything is Ready

LUKE 14:15–24

Go out into the streets and lanes of the town and bring in the poor, the crippled, the blind and the lame.

How could anyone in their right senses refuse the gospel invitation which Jesus gives to the wedding feast? Here is an open welcome to love, joy and peace, yet there are those who remain hostile, indifferent, or simply do not seem to hear. I have known some people turn away because they think the feast is dull. They look at the professing Church, they see through the hypocritical and double-dealing lives of some of its members, and they observe the lacklustre or bigoted and exclusivist lifestyles, and say, 'Not for me, thank you!' Then I have known some who hear the invitation as a threat. It comes over as 'Come to Jesus – for if you don't you will burn in hell for ever!' Who can blame them for treading such an invitation underfoot? If the nature and character of God is that of a tyrant and despot, then they will look elsewhere for the fulfilment of their deepest yearnings.

I have some friends who cannot accept the invitation because it is too good to be true. They tell me that I seem to have found great joy and peace, that it has given me a dimension to life that they envy, and that they only wish it were true. They do not, of course, believe that I am out to deceive them, but that I have believed in a vision which has originated in the minds of the greatest and truest souls down the ages. But they look at the chaos, the cruelty, the injustice and inhumanity of our suffering world, and cannot believe in a God of love.

Some of these people give their lives in loving service to others. They are people of dedication and sacrifice. I believe they will be gently carried into the kingdom of God protesting with glad amazement, 'When was it that we saw you hungry and gave you food, or thirsty and gave you drink . . . naked and clothed you . . . sick or in prison and visited you?' And the Lord will answer them, 'Truly I tell you, just as you did it to one of the least of these . . . you did it to me.' (Matthew 25:37-40)

It is strange how scripture can be interpreted to fulfil our own projected ideas of what God and the Gospel is. *Compelle intrare*, 'Compel them to come in' (v 23) are words which have been used to impose a stark decree of predestination which can have a double edge to it, and has also been used to force non-Christian armies to convert, or as a text for the persecution of one section of the Church by another. Shades of the Crusades! This is certainly not what Jesus had in mind. And yet there *is* a kind of divine compulsion which arises from the experience of the sinner who feels scales fall from his eyes, or the veil lift from her heart.

There are areas in my own life in which I have tried to live apart from God, but relationships have deteriorated, coveted possessions have turned to dust and ambitions have been thwarted. Through my life I have experienced God compelling me to realize all this, gently pushing (or pulling) me into relationships or situations which I would not have chosen but which have turned out to be fulfilling, exciting and joyful. There are even situations which have yielded pain and darkness, but have been necessary for my human and spiritual maturity. C. S. Lewis puts it like this:

> The Prodigal Son at least walked home on his own feet. But who can duly adore that Love which will open the high gates to a prodigal who is brought in kicking, struggling, resentful and darting his eyes in every direction for a chance of escape? The words *compelle intrare*, compel them to come in, have been so abused by wicked men that we shudder at them. But, properly understood they plumb the depth of the Divine Mercy. The hardness of God is kinder than the softness of men, and his compulsion is our liberation. (*Surprised by Joy*)

But there is also a warning. It is that those who are invited can refuse so often that they no longer hear the invitation, and lock themselves out of the wedding feast. It does not mean the punishment of an everlasting, burning hell, but it does mean eternal loss. For if a person turns away from love, light and life, it means a lapse, a falling into lostness, darkness and ultimate non-being. This, of course, implies that the sinner purposely, knowingly, maliciously, looks into the face of the divine Love and rejects the offer of life and forgiveness.

What about the parable's ordinary excuses? Can they be so culpable, and is it possible to fall away from the kingdom of

God so easily? Well, look at them again, and consider how constant choices of the second-best can lead a person further and further from the loving Father who cries, 'Come, for everything is ready.'

PRAYER

Master of the Gospel feast:
You have set before us the joys, the liberties and the loving
    communion of the Gospel of Christ;
You have invited us to the bread of sharing and the sweet
    wine of rejoicing.
Let us not keep our eyes lowered to the level of material
    gain and marketplace values, but let the sheer joy and
    excitement of the celebration of all life fill our earthly
    days with gladness;
And let it all be consummated at last in the kingdom of
    God. Amen.

RESPONSE

Look at the excuses in the parable, and ask if they are also yours:
1. 'I have bought a piece of land.' Property, wealth, investments, real estate.
2. 'I have bought five yoke of oxen.' Ambition, avarice, technological expertise, power and influence over others, reputation, commercial exploitation.

3. 'I have just been married.' Relationships, success, comfort, domestic ease, flaunting sexuality, economic selfishness.

Of course, these areas may not only be legitimate, but may well glorify God if they are within his will. But used as excuses to keep God at bay they can become betrayals of love and lead to emptiness. Living in the will of God redeems all other dimensions of life. Ask yourself if your life is humanly fulfilled and what relation it has to the will and love of God.

Groups
Share with other members the sort of area in your life which could be subject to these excuses, and any experience you may have had of God gently compelling you in a certain direction.

LENT 2
Jesus, Man of Wonders

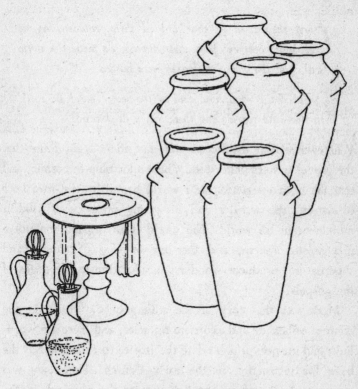

Do whatever he tells you

Lent 2: Sunday

Cosmic Lord

PSALM 107:23-30; MARK 4:35-41

Then they cried to the Lord in their trouble, and he brought them out from their distress; he made the storm be still, and the waves of the sea were hushed.

He rebuked the wind, and said to the sea, 'Peace! Be still!'
Then the wind ceased, and there was a dead calm.

Whatever secular theologians may say, there is no doubt that the gospel writers understood Christ's lordship as cosmic, and that far from interfering in a world bound by cast-iron laws of nature, the wonder and life-giving presence of God is immanent in his world. The world is an organic and not a mechanistic system, and the interweaving of natural and supernatural produces wonder and adoration in the pages of the gospels.

Mark sets the story of the stilling of the storm in the context of healing and exorcism miracles, and there are word-links and nuances which relate the stories to each other as the basis for instruction in the early Church. This story was meant to be heard by the believers at the eucharist in the context of the worship of Christ as Saviour and Cosmic Lord.

The troubled and restless sea was always a sphere of danger, mystery and terror to the Hebrew mind, symbolizing the fearful and sinful world: 'The wicked are like the tossing sea that cannot keep still; its waters toss up mire and mud.' (Isaiah 57:20) The only one who can still the raging torrents which threaten to engulf the terrified mariner is God himself. This is set out beautifully and powerfully in Psalm 107. The application would be clear to the listener, and a typical interpretation is found in Tertullian's text on baptism:

> That little ship presented a figure of the Church, in that she is disquieted in the sea, that is, in the world, by the waves, that is, by persecutions and temptations, the Lord patiently sleeping, as it were, until, roused at last by the prayers of the saints, he checks the world and restores tranquillity to his own.

Some of the listeners to this Marcan passage were living in Rome during the days of Emperor Nero's persecution. It encouraged them to affirm the Lord's presence when tempted to think that he was indifferent or asleep. When things were in desperate straits, then the Lord would arise in the boat, rebuke and silence the wind and waves, and restore the peace of God in the human heart and in the boat of the persecuted Church.

Mark also seems to be indicating that the powers of darkness were at work in this storm, for the words that Jesus uses are the same that are used in the exorcism of the demon-possessed man in the synagogue at Capernaum. They occur in Mark 1:25, and are repeated in our passage, Mark 4:39:

epetimèse (he rebuked)

pephimòso (be muzzled)

Both the demon and the storm were rebuked, and the man and the elements were exorcised and still. Christ the Lord of humankind and of the world he has made brought peace. In an eighth-century hymn by Anatolius, he pictures the ferocity of the storm and darkness, the wailing of the wind, and the labour and terror of the mariners. The final stanza is a cry to the Saviour in life and death:

Jesu, Deliverer,
   Near to us be;
Soothe thou my voyaging
   Over life's sea;
Thou, when the storms of death
   Roars, sweeping by,
Whisper, O Truth of truth,
   'Peace! It is I.'

PRAYER

Christ Jesus, Lord of creation:
You hold the world in the hollow of your hand; you still the
   raging sea and contain the wildness of the storm.
When I am attacked by sickness, persecuted by those who
   would beat me down, and laid low by my mortality in
   the valley of the shadow, hear my prayer.

*Arise in my heart and rebuke the enemy, deliver me from the
final death and bring me to the desired haven of your
heavenly kingdom.* Amen.

RESPONSE

Sit in quietness and read or sing over the hymn 'Fierce raged
the tempest o'er the deep', imagining yourself within the
story told by Mark. Enter into Christ's peace.

Groups

Sit around a central candle in an otherwise dark room, and
let one member read the story, followed by the playing over
of the hymn (tune: St Aelred) on flute or piano, etc. Follow
with fifteen minutes of silence, and depart for home with no
further conversation.

Lent 2: Monday

Demons, Disease and Death

MARK 5:1–43

Jesus said to him, 'Go home to your friends, and tell them how much the Lord has done for you, and what mercy he has shown you.'

He said to her, 'Daughter, your faith has made you well; go in peace, and be healed of your disease.'

He took her by the hand and said, 'Little girl, get up.' And immediately the girl got up and began to walk about (she was twelve years of age).

Yesterday we thought of Jesus as Cosmic Lord over the elements, and the disciples' awesome response, 'Who then is this, that even the wind and the sea obey him?' Today, Mark presents to us in a telescoped passage three interrelated miracles of healing, showing not only Jesus' power over demons, disease and death, but also his loving embrace of the whole of our humanity. In this section he exorcises the man, heals the woman, and raises the child.

The poor man was out of his mind, possessed with madness, and when Jesus forced the evil spirit to speak, using the man's voice, he cried out, 'My name is Legion, for we are many.' The only answer his society would give to this situation of spiritual darkness and mental schizophrenia was restraint with chains and shackles, because they were afraid. Jesus comes with calm confidence and unfailing compassion. He found the man crying, bleeding, suffering among the tombs, and left him seated, clothed and in his right mind (v 15). The text says the people, because of their fear, begged Jesus to leave the region. They were more afraid of Jesus than of the demoniac, for they realized what power he had.

So Jesus crossed the lake and was soon surrounded by a needy crowd. He was completely available to God, therefore ready to meet a crowd or an individual. So when Jairus came to him in extremity, and cried out, 'My little daughter . . .' Jesus immediately went with him. As Mark telescopes the story, we are soon introduced to the woman who tremblingly draws near to Jesus as he accompanies Jairus. She had suffered for twelve years from a chronic haemorrhage which was not only debilitating and left her penniless, but also excluded her from social and religious fellowship. She heard of Jesus, and cherished a flicker of faith, even if it had superstitious overtones. But she came believing.

It is a wonderful portrayal of reaching out in utter yearning; touching, feeling a surge of dynamic power, with the complete assurance of healing. I say 'dynamic power' because the text says that Jesus was aware that power (*dunamis*) had gone forth from him (v 30), and *dunamis* is the origin of our word dynamite!

Breaking in upon this healing came messengers to say that the child was dead. In the face of Jairus' devastation, Jesus said, 'Do not fear, only believe.' Then he took Peter, James and John and went into the house. He rebuked the mourners, silenced their unbelief, and put them outside. Then with the three disciples and the child's parents he went into the room where she was lying, tenderly took her hand, and we hear the very words which Jesus spoke in the Aramaic tongue: '*Talitha cum*'. We only have three occasions when we hear the *very words* of Jesus, and this is one of them. Little wonder at the reaction of the people when the girl responded to Jesus' life-giving words. I like the awkward but literal translation of the King James' Bible: 'And they were astonished with a great astonishment.'

This chapter is packed with spiritual and practical insights into the human condition, and at every turn Mark is showing us the wonder, the sympathy, the power and the universal embrace of Jesus as the Messiah. Mark is sometimes secretive about this Messiah role (v 43). Jesus is not to be the military warrior who delivers his people with a bloody massacre or political genius, but the suffering Saviour, whose power is that of gentle compassion, healing and the call to a radical discipleship of the heart.

PRAYER

Healing Christ:
Your arms were open to men, women and children; your
  power was displayed in mental, physical and spiritual
  healing.
Filled with astonishment and humbled in adoration I
  acknowledge your mercy.

Begin a new work of healing in me today, Lord, and enable
me with open mind and heart to embrace all those who
need your life-giving touch. Amen.

RESPONSE

Reflecting upon our stories today, do you know of anyone
with psychiatric problems, a physical disease, or in bereavement where your word, your visit, your practical help could
channel the compassion of Christ into their lives? Then make
that visit, write that letter, take that job in hand, in the name
of Christ.

Groups

As a result of your personal reflection you may be able to
pool your findings with the group and see if there may be
corporate or 'team' ways to help sufferers or carers in the
neighbourhood, so that the church may more truly represent
its Lord.

Lent 2: Tuesday

Wine that Makes the Heart Glad

PSALM 104:14-15; JOHN 2:1-11

*Y*ou cause the grass to grow for the cattle, and plants for
the people to use, to bring forth food from the earth, and
wine to gladden the human heart, oil to make the face shine,
and bread to strengthen the human heart.*

*'Everyone serves the good wine first, and then the inferior wine.
But you have kept the good wine until now.' Jesus did this,
the first of his signs, in Cana of Galilee, and revealed his
glory; and his disciples believed in him.*

I was brought up in a church which taught teetotalism, and
sermons were preached on such texts from the King James'
Bible as 'Wine is a mocker, strong drink is raging: and
whosoever is deceived thereby is not wise' (Proverbs 20:1),
and 'Look not upon the wine when it is red . . . at the last
it biteth like a serpent, and stingeth like an adder.' (Proverbs
23:31-32) In the Methodist Sunday School we were given
temperance leaflets called 'Wideawakes Own', and in the
Baptist 'Band of Hope', at ten years of age I recited: 'I promise, by divine assistance, to abstain from all intoxicating
liquor, and to encourage others to do the same.' I'm still a
teetotaller, and this is one of the things I learned in the

church which Jesus never taught! I don't think the writer of Proverbs was an abstainer, but rather a remorseful imbiber!

The fact is that wine (though not drunkenness) symbolizes gladness, and the fact that Jesus is at the heart of this story of celebration means that he is the provider of joy – the one who transforms situations of sadness and embarrassment into experiences of gladness and rejoicing.

There is a mingling of joy and sorrow through the experience of the pre-Easter disciples, but once they had caught sight of the risen Christ and opened their minds and hearts to his immortal life, then joy and gladness sprang up in their hearts. When Jesus appeared to the anxious and defeated disciples in the locked upper room, the text says, 'Then the disciples rejoiced when they saw the Lord.' (John 20:20) From that moment on, in times of blessing or persecution there was a deep source of joy in their hearts because the risen Christ dwelt within. So here, in the miracle story of the transformation of water into wine, there is an anticipation of the joy of the kingdom of God.

I worked, during one Christmas vacation, at a hotel in Chateau D'Oex in Switzerland, with a dozen or so international students. We had a party at the end of the working holiday in our skivvy chalet, and when most of the group brought bottles, I provided food. 'Oh, you don't need liquor,' quipped one of the lads with a grin, 'you're tipsy all the time.' I hope he meant I was inebriated with joy, because that is what this story is about.

Notice the attitude of Mary in it all. First of all she was not perturbed by the anxiety and shame of the wine running out – she simply turned instinctively to Jesus. His answer, at face value, seems strange and ambiguous, but without completely understanding, she trusted him completely to do what was necessary. Then she turned to the servants and said, 'Do whatever he tells you.' Perhaps there are some lessons here which we may learn with our Lord's mother:

1. Share with Jesus in the joyful and human celebration of ordinary life.
2. Turn to him instinctively whenever we are confronted by sorrow, perplexity or fear.
3. Trust him implicitly whether we understand his working in our life, or not.
4. Point others to a similar trust and joy in following him.

The result of this first of the miracle signs in John's gospel was a consolidation of the disciples' faith, and a radiance which suffused the wedding feast at Cana in Galilee.

PRAYER

Jesus, Master of the feast:
You are the bringer of new wine, the provider of joy and
*   gladness;*
Melancholy and despair have no part in your saving Gospel,
*   so forgive your people for taking their eyes from you and*
*   living in the valley of depression and fear.*
Lift our eyes and hearts to glimpse your glory, and may our
*   lives radiate the inebriating joy of God. Amen.*

RESPONSE

First ask around your circle of non-Christian friends and
workmates whether they think of committed Christians as
people of joy or despondency, affirming or negating life in the
world. Then ask them what differences they would expect in
someone who professes to follow Christ.

Share your findings with your group, and listen to what the
other members relate. Do the results surprise you? What kind
of action is needed as a result of this investigation? How about
sharing it with the clergy and wider congregation?

Lent 2: Wednesday

From the Mountain to the Valley

EXODUS 34:29-35; MARK 9:14-29

They brought the boy to Jesus. When the spirit saw him it immediately convulsed the boy, and he fell on the ground and rolled about, foaming at the mouth. Jesus asked the father, 'How long has this been happening to him?'

And he said, 'From childhood. It has often cast him into the fire and into the water, to destroy him; but if you are able to do anything, have pity on us and help us.'

Jesus said to him, ' "If you are able!" All things can be done for the one who believes.' Immediately the father of the child cried out, 'I believe; help my unbelief!'

The wonder, the drama, the pain and the yearning of this episode is depicted in Raphael's famous *Transfiguration* painting. In the upper portion of the painting the splendour and ecstasy of the transfigured Christ is portrayed, with Moses and Elijah on either side, and the three dazed disciples shielding their eyes from the radiant glory. In the lower portion a furious theological confrontation is taking place between gesticulating disciples and ecclesiastics, while the epileptic boy, contorted and rigid, is held by the poor father whose staring eyes and anguished face reveal the tragedy of the situation.

When Jesus appeared, the crowd was immediately overcome with awe. Perhaps they traced the lingering transfiguration glory on the face of Jesus, as had happened with Moses so many centuries before. Into the chaos of controversy and impotence of the crowd, the ecclesiastics, and the nine impotent disciples below, comes Jesus with the light and glory of the mountain shining in his very being. He asks, 'What are you arguing about?' It becomes clear. The poor man relates the sad story of the evil spirit that from childhood has seized and tormented his boy, and the disappointment at the inability of the disciples to help him.

This is an old story. So often, against the evil spirits of war and bloodshed, the economic chasm between rich and poor, against racial inequalities and the abuses of power, the Church has been impotent, because it has been caught up in the shame of it all itself. In Umberto Eco's *The Name of the Rose*, in the midst of the poverty, disease and helplessness of thirteenth-century Europe, and with the spectre of murder within the monastery itself, the monks are involved in doctrinal disputation, inquisition and mutual persecution. It is said that in 1917, in the same Moscow street in which revolutionary bloodshed was being planned, there was a meeting of church prelates arguing over vestments and liturgy! So it has continued down the centuries, is around us today, and in your heart and mine, while the Christ says in both pity and judgement, 'You faithless generation, how much longer must I put up with you?'

At this moment in the text, the power of God breaks in.

The boy is brought to Jesus, convulsing, rolling about, foaming and crying. The father cries out in anguish, 'If you are able, have pity . . . and help.' Jesus takes up the plea, affirms the power of God, calls forth the man's faith, and the man cries out again in words which shake our very souls if we are at all moved by the reality of this human dilemma of suffering and hope: 'I believe; help my unbelief!' And he does. Jesus authoritatively commands the evil spirit to come out for ever, and with crying and convulsions the boy seems drained of colour and life – the crowd think he is dead. But Jesus takes hold of the boy's hand, as he had done with Jairus' daughter, and restores him to his father.

The Jesus who did this mighty work is the One who has gazed upon the unutterable glory of the Father on the mountain, who has been irradiated by the light and splendour of the Spirit of God, and who has communed in prayer and adoration in the light of his coming cross and passion. The path to such healing and compassionate power is through the way of prayer and communion with God. Only by gazing upon the glory of God on the mountain will we be enabled to live and love in the valley, enabling the radiance of God's light to shine in the darkness of the valley below.

PRAYER

Christ of light and glory:
Upon the holy mountain you were transfigured in the
presence and radiance of the Father;

In the dark valley you channelled the healing compassion of
  your loving heart.
Grant that I may be open to the Father in my utter need,
  and to humankind in lowly service and understanding,
  that your will may be done in the valley, as it is upon
  the mountain. Amen.

RESPONSE

If you can find a reproduction of Raphael's *Transfiguration*, place it before you, with a candle burning, and read through the whole transfiguration and healing story in today's scripture.

How much time and energy have you spent in the last year involving yourself in fruitless arguments and verbose confrontations? Is the time spent proportionate to that spent in the secret place of prayer?

Put it to the test this Lent. Spend some special time holding up a particular person or situation to God, and then, if your heart tells you, go gently and sensitively to that person or situation, allowing God to use you as the channel of his healing love.

Share the outcome with members of your group; listen to the experiences of the others; learn from one another.

Lent 2: Thursday

Let Me See Again

MARK 10:46-52; HEBREWS 12:1-2

*Throwing off his cloak, he sprang up and came to Jesus.
Then Jesus said to him, 'What do you want me to do for
you?' The blind man said, 'My teacher, let me see again.'*

*Let us lay aside every weight and the sin that clings so closely,
and let us run with perseverance the race that is set before us,
looking to Jesus the pioneer and perfector of our faith.*

'Let me see again.' What hope and yearning are expressed in
those few words from blind Bartimaeus from Jericho. These
days at the beginning of Lent in my hermitage are proving to
be days of vision, and I thank God for my sight. Yesterday
the spring sunshine broke through, shining upon the clumps
of snowdrops around my enclosure; the buds and leaves are
multiplying every day; and I have just received, by post, a gift
of various potted fuchsias with a warning not to put them
outside until there is less fear of hard frost. This morning
there was ice inside and outside my hut, and though the
luscious green grass sweeps down to the woodland below, it
began to snow an hour or so ago and the wind is rushing
through the trees all about me. I can see it all, as I write

about a poor blind man. What an appealing story it is, and how I appreciate my sight.

Mark is the racy gospel writer who keeps things moving, and I like the dramatic way he has of telling stories. The blind beggar is described by two sets of verbs, with Jesus 'standing still' between them. The beggar sat/begged/heard/cried/ persisted. Then Jesus stood still and called him. He then cast aside his cloak/rose/came/responded/saw/and followed. This is the last miracle that Mark records, for Jesus is just fifteen miles from Jerusalem and the burden of the cross is already upon him. Yet, though his mind and heart are given to that journey, here, just beside the way, is one sad individual who needs him.

We don't know anything of the man's background, but the fact that he wanted to see *again* indicates that at some point he had lost the gift of sight. How many years had he sat begging in darkness? How many memories of days that used to be must have haunted his days and nights? The story is told succinctly in the old gospel song, and a pointed application made:

One sat alone beside the highway begging,
His eyes were blind, the light he could not see;
He clutched his rags, and shivered in the shadows,
Then Jesus came — and bade the darkness flee.

When Jesus comes, the tempter's power is broken,
When Jesus comes, the tears are wiped away;
He takes the gloom, and fills the life with glory,
For all is changed — when Jesus comes to stay.

I am the first to affirm the simple and joyful application of the gospel in this evangelical style. But the trouble is that it sometimes sounds so slick and easy when an evangelist is describing it. The blind man himself would not have been as slick. He would have spoken of days of darkness, and nights awake in yearning. He would have recounted feelings of re-dundance and uselessness, the loss of vision and manhood, of being reduced to poverty and begging, and perhaps years of unanswered prayer. He would also have told of that moment when he heard that Jesus was nearby; of his shouting, demanding, repeating, 'Jesus, Son of David, have mercy on me!' The effect of such wholehearted and persistent crying was that Jesus stood still.

I find in the dark morning hour prayers, wrapped in my cloak against the early cold, that I repeat the *Jesus Prayer* for myself, for those in pain and terminal illness, and for our poor world: 'Lord Jesus Christ, Son of God, have mercy . . .' There are times when I feel that Jesus stands still – listening simply to me. My shouting turns to awe and wonder as I feel him say to me as he said to blind Bartimaeus, 'What do you want me to do for you?'

For Bartimaeus it meant becoming quiet, repeating gently the deepest desire of his heart, and opening himself com-pletely to receive the healing vision that only Jesus can give. But all this only after Bartimaeus had cast away the cloak of his hindrances, and sought Jesus only.

This very morning, in temperatures below freezing, I prayed for the cold and naked children of Bosnia, and especially Sarajevo, as I was wrapped around with the cloak that Brother Amos has given me for this winter. My hindrances, longings, helplessness and desire for a renewal of vision mingles with the story of Bartimaeus at this point in Lent. Like him, I want to respond to the touch of Jesus, be renewed in vision, and follow to my life's end.

PRAYER

Jesus, who makes the blind see:
I am as lacking in vision, as helpless in need, as Bartimaeus
on the road to Jericho.
On the way to Calvary you stood still to listen to him, just
as you stand before me now with great patience and
affection.
Listen to me today, aid my helplessness, help me to cast
away the cloak of my sins and hindrances that block my
sight, and renew my vision so that I may follow you with
all my heart. Amen.

RESPONSE

Know that Jesus can meet the very need that you feel in yourself today, and for those you hold in faith and prayer. Are there barriers to blessing, hindrances to grace, sins of obstruction in your life that prevent his blessing and healing flowing?

As Christ stands still before you today, let him search the deep places in your heart, showing you those things which hinder and grieve his Holy Spirit. Then 'cast away your cloak' and surrender to his love, thereby releasing the spring of blessing and grace.

Lent 2: Friday

Bent Double

LUKE 13:10-17

'*You hypocrites! Does not each of you on the Sabbath untie his ox or his donkey from the manger, and lead it away to give it water? And ought not this woman, a daughter of Abraham, whom Satan bound for eighteen long years, be set free from this bondage on the Sabbath day?' When he said this, all his opponents were put to shame, and the entire crowd was rejoicing at all the wonderful things that he was doing.*

In my early Sunday School days we were set region-wide and somewhat competitive scripture examinations. I diligently pored over narrative, poetry, parables and miracle stories, imbibing the letter of scripture and learning great chunks of it by heart. Most of my knowledge of the content of scripture dates from those days, and some images impressed themselves on my mind indelibly – among which was this woman 'bent double' for eighteen years. Much of my love for Jesus was ignited by the sympathy which saw, reached out, and restored such a parody of what a whole, straight and healthy life should be.

My first reading of scripture was not as a theological undergraduate in the critics' den (that came later), but as a child, and that child came to 'know' this Jesus of whom the evangelists wrote. My experience of Jesus, 'the same yesterday, today and for ever', was communicated through the gospels by the power of the Holy Spirit. The Spirit who inspired the writers also inspired the reader, and evoked in me the same response. Therefore, having learned from the text and the Spirit, I was able to profit from an objective and critical theological education without losing the immediacy, the reality and the joy of the saving, healing Christ. So, in coming to such a story as this, with all my critical awareness and at least some theological maturity, I still feel that leap of recognition of the same Jesus who met me in the pages of scripture so many decades ago. And he is still the same.

Nevertheless, the fact that this woman presented the problem of human suffering which had persisted for eighteen years as one among many other sufferers, also makes me realize the rarity of such miracles, as well as the reality of them. I think of one of our former friars who was himself bent almost double with a spinal malformation. He was confronted, one day, with a superficial fundamentalist fellow, who thought himself God's gift to the Church. 'Do you want to be healed?' he asked the old friar, with a self-styled authority that the old man perceived. 'No!' came the sure and sharp reply. The friar was not answering the gospel question, but a fundamentalist question which was filled with presumption and a lack of discernment. During this week's reading of miracle stories, we must be open to the forgiving and healing power of Christ, and also to the fact that many people do not receive physical healing, yet live near to the heart of God, and themselves become wounded healers in their ministry to others.

There was a group of religionists in this story who were more concerned with theological legalisms than with the compassion which prompted Jesus to lay his hands of healing upon this poor woman. They would have stoned adulterers, burned witches and excommunicated sinners. Jesus broke their rules but kept the law of love, upset their regulations but fulfilled his Father's commandment.

The woman was bent double. Jesus called her, spoke tenderly to her, laid his hands upon her, straightened her and set her completely free, upright and praising God. And that, in turn, set the people rejoicing and praising too. It spreads like wildfire!

PRAYER

Lord Jesus, liberator of captives:

You enabled this poor woman to straighten her spine, so that her eyes could be raised to the sun;

You ended the suffering of her eighteen years, and caused her to enter into her inheritance as a daughter of Abraham and a child of faith.

Grant that I may stand straight today, lifting my eyes from the base things of earth, to gaze into your face of sympathy and joy;

Then those around will have reason to rejoice too, thereby releasing the spirit of praise and hope in our dark world. Amen.

RESPONSE

Today's questions may be put to you personally or to the group sharing together after personal reflection.

Put yourself into the story and examine any attitudes of bigotry and legalism which may be part of your religious profession. Do any of the characters in the story reflect your own experience and outlook? Are you caught up in any kind of spiritual, moral or physical bondage that calls for liberation? Are you bowed down with anxiety, addictions, wrong relationships that have bound you over the years? Do you shield yourself from real love and compassion by a religion of rules and regulations, with a bigoted and exclusivist spirit?

Are you one of the crowd rejoicing in the salvation/healing of others but never having experienced personal relationship with Christ for yourself? Be open for a complete loosening of your bonds, straightening of your spine, liberation of your whole outlook.

Lent 2: Saturday

Jesus Wept

JOHN 11:1-44

When Mary came where Jesus was and saw him, she knelt at his feet and said to him, 'Lord, if you had been here, my brother would not have died.'

When Jesus saw her weeping, and the Jews who came with her also weeping, he was greatly disturbed in spirit and deeply moved. He said, 'Where have you laid him?'

They said to him, 'Lord, come and see.' Jesus began to weep. So the Jews said, 'See how he loved him!' But some of them said, 'Could not he who opened the eyes of the blind man have kept this man from dying?'

Things can suddenly change. Bereavement can overtake us in a moment. A few days ago I was writing about the spring sunshine, the budding of lilac and viburnum trees, and the thrusting up of daffodils into the warming February air. This morning at 5.00 I opened my hut door and was greeted by the silent, white world of insulating snow, with not a bud or plant to be seen. It is snowing furiously as I write of the stark and wintry contrast of profound, loving relationships and sudden, fearful bereavement.

Well I remember the preparation for the procession at Glasshampton monastery on the feast of the Presentation of Christ in the Temple, on 2 February 1988. The telephone rang and I answered, to hear that my father had suddenly died without warning. I returned home for the funeral. My sister and I felt the deep sorrow of his death as we comforted my mother and encouraged her to share in love and hope with us as we looked forward to spring. But before the end of the month, as we entered into Lent, she also died suddenly. I looked down into the grave on a bleak day, for the second time within a month and felt the immediate truth of what C. S. Lewis recorded anonymously in his melancholic and yet beautiful book *A Grief Observed*, which was the result of the death of his wife Joy.

I don't want to meditate this morning on the wonder of the raising of Lazarus because our bereavements are not usually resolved in such a supernatural manner. Don't get me wrong, John believed that Jesus actually raised Lazarus from physical death and saw it in the light of the resurrection of Jesus. But he is writing as an evangelist and not as an historian, and he does not encourage his readers to claim the raising of their departed loved ones. Rather he points us to the immense sadness that engulfed the community at Bethany, the two sisters Mary and Martha, and which drew Jesus into its close embrace of sorrow, aching and weeping, The wonder is not that Jesus restored Lazarus to his sisters, but that he could enter at such depth of grief and mourning into their bereavement, and thus share universal bereavement. As he wept for Lazarus, he grieved, groaned and cried for the dying of all creation.

85

Jesus was the second Adam, the Cosmic Lord, the self-emptied Logos who became human in that amazing movement of incarnation at Bethlehem. He felt our earthly sorrows with more, not less, intensity. He entered more deeply into the woes and pains of our human situation in its finitude, subject to the bondage of decay and death. As with much of my deepest understanding of the Gospel, I glimpsed this as a child through Bishop William Walsham How's hymn:

It is a thing most wonderful,
  Almost too wonderful to be,
That God's own Son should come from heaven
  And die to save a child like me.

And yet I know that it is true:
  He came to this poor world below,
And wept and toiled and mourned and died,
  Only because he loved us so.

I've just checked this hymn in a modern hymn book, and find that they have removed the words 'wept' and 'mourned'. Why this fear of allowing the grieving, sorrowing Jesus to meet our need? There are times when I need the God who weeps, not the God who reigns!

'See how he loved him', was the response of the community at Bethany when they saw the tears of Jesus at the grave of his friend. And they went on: 'Could he not . . . have kept this man from dying?' Yes, he could have – but he did not. For something even more wonderful was in store. This did not prevent the grief, the mourning, the weeping, but at the last it revealed the amazing grace which will reconcile all things through the eternal Love.

The snow is still falling thickly as I end this reflection today. I know that the leaves and buds, the thrusting bulbs and even the aquadulce beans are beneath the snow, but as Lent gives way to Easter I shall be surrounded by the warmth and wonder of yet another spring.

PRAYER

Lord Jesus who weeps with your people:

There is no pain or sorrow that you have not felt more keenly; there is no sickness or bereavement that you have not entered more intensely; there is no depth of darkness that you have not plumbed.

Help us in our bereavements of body and spirit to share in your tears as you share in ours, and grant that we may share in that life which is beyond all pain. Amen.

RESPONSE

Think of a friend or neighbour who has recently suffered personal bereavement. Spend some time holding them in faith and love before God, and then sensitively visit or write as seems appropriate, and (with their permission) include them in the intercessions at the eucharist on Sunday.

LENT 3

Jesus, Man for Sinners

Zacchaeus climbed a tree
to see Jesus

Lent 3: Sunday

Vertically Challenged

LUKE 19:1-10

Jesus entered Jericho and was passing through it. A man was there named Zacchaeus; he was a chief tax collector and was rich. He was trying to see who Jesus was, but on account of the crowd he could not, because he was short in stature.

If Zacchaeus was vertically challenged it was not because he was short of stature but because he climbed up a tree! The challenge of Jesus came to him not because he was hiding in the crowd but because he was hiding among the foliage of the tree, but still curious.

This is an interesting story because Zacchaeus was a big man in terms of his money, and a small man in terms of his reputation – but before the story is out the situation is radically changed. The day started out like any other, for Zacchaeus did not know that Jesus had determined to confront him in unusual circumstances with amazing results. He did not know that he would shin up a tree, forgetting his dignity, nor that he would lose half his fortune immediately and dole out the rest to those he had previously defrauded.

The name Zacchaeus means pure, or righteous, though his life belied his name. But his mother may have rejoiced if she had known that he would become, if the *Clementine Homilies* are correct, the Bishop of Caesarea!

There were a few things of which we are certain – that he was rich, that he was short, and that he was lonely. But he was also curious. Or was it his conscience and his loneliness that caused him to want to see Jesus? Perhaps he had heard of Jesus' reputation of consorting with tax collectors (Luke 5:30). His loneliness was brought about by his traitorous job, collecting taxes on behalf of a repressive, occupying regime, with the defrauding that went on wholesale with such a job. Many of his countrymen despised him, rating him as a robber, an informant or a brothel-keeper. Tax collectors and sinners were lumped together. His money only widened the gap, and perhaps in the evenings the money was his only friend.

So what was in his mind and heart as that day began? Certainly he was searching, and his quest had to do with Jesus. The matter had become so important that he overcame the obstacles of height and secrecy, in climbing among the sycamore foliage. Here was a man seeking God, not knowing that God has already determined to find *him*! That is how grace works. We only seek God because we have already been found by him. We can only repent because we have already received the grace of the Holy Spirit, for

Every virtue we possess, and every victory won,
And every thought of holiness are his alone.

Zacchaeus was in his place before Jesus arrived – but Jesus

91

knew. When Jesus came directly under the tree, Zacchaeus strained to see him. Suddenly he was looking into Jesus' eyes, and heard Jesus invite himself to Zacchaeus' house, into Zacchaeus' heart, into Zacchaeus' life: 'Zacchaeus, hurry and come down; for I must stay at your house today.'

Now here is the part of the story I would most want to learn. Just *what* did Jesus say to Zacchaeus, and what did Zacchaeus ask, say, reply to Jesus? I suspect that when he looked into the eyes of Jesus from his hiding place he saw the man he might have been, could have been, should have been – and could be. I suspect that Zacchaeus poured out his heart's loneliness to Jesus; that he had come short in stature, in relationships, in moral standards, in love for his fellows. Perhaps it all stemmed from his loneliness and inadequacy as a child, and led to a lack of esteem that made him avaricious of 'things' because he lacked in love.

Perhaps there were tears. Certainly a hard and avaricious heart was melted, a lonely and yearning quest was answered, and all this needed to happen behind the privacy of closed doors, not while Zacchaeus was perched over the heads of the people. While they were inside, the people began to grumble, for Zacchaeus' reputation was not a savoury one, and it was difficult for them to understand why the prophet had invited himself into such a morally doubtful situation. But the Saviour had done his work, and transformation was complete and ongoing as the amazed audience heard that the avaricious tax collector was immediately giving half his possessions to the poor, and in obedience to Mosaic law would make a fourfold restitution to any he had defrauded (Exodus 22:1).

The invitation of Jesus is always the same, yet tailor-made

to personal need: 'Come to me you that are weary and are carrying heavy burdens, and I will give you rest.' (Matthew 11:28) Jesus affirmed that Zacchaeus was a true son of Abraham, setting out into the unknown by faith (Hebrews 11:8-10), and their joy mingled, for Jesus had sought and found one who had been lost.

He is not a disappointment,
Jesus is far more to me
Than in all my glowing daydreams
I'd imagined he could be;
And the more I get to know him
So the more I find him true,
And the more I long that others
Should be led to know him too.

PRAYER

Jesus, seeker and Saviour of the lost:
You found little Zacchaeus in an unusual place, and restored
to him the dignity, the compassion and the love he had
traded away.
If you have appointed a meeting with me today, let me
clearly hear your invitation, hurry down from my secret
hiding-place, and give you your place in my home, in my
heart, in my life. Amen.

RESPONSE

Do you know anyone generally disliked, whom you also dislike? Perhaps because of his or her avarice, meanness, malice or hardness of heart? Have you wondered about the roots of the problem, of how much they long for love, for friendship, for warmth?

Fix upon them in prayer over a period of time and ask the Lord to soften your heart, give you discernment. Then if the way opens up, gently and sensitively make the right approach at the right time. All this in the light of the story of Zacchaeus.

Lent 3: Monday

Caught in the Act

JOHN 8:1-11

The scribes and the Pharisees brought a woman who had been caught in adultery; and making her stand before all of them, they said to him, 'Teacher, this woman was caught in the very act of committing adultery. In the Law Moses commanded us to stone such women. Now what do you say?' They said this to test him, so that they might have some charge to bring against him.

Do we sometimes have to be theologically wrong in order to be pastorally right? Or is it that pastoral discernment which is governed by compassion (not sentimentality) at the last leads us to understand our theology aright?

Both Catholics and Protestants have agreed with the burning of witches, and both slavery and apartheid have been justified on biblical grounds. There are some sects which allow loved ones to die rather than receive blood transfusions, and others will not allow their own children or parents to eat with them because they are not 'orthodox'. All this is based on a theological interpretation of scripture. When we realize that nearly all the sects believe in the infallibility of the Bible, yet radically disagree about its interpretation, it

95

should make us cautious about our own claims.

You see how much of a hornet's nest can be stirred up by today's passage? Perhaps it is not surprising that it is a 'floating passage'. Many of the earliest and best manuscripts do not have it at all. Some include it at the end of John, and some after Luke 21:38. But here it is, clearly embedded in the received text, and it is pastorally necessary for the Church of God.

The first thing we are faced with is the callousness of the Pharisees who forced this poor woman to stand in front of them all. They didn't care about her or about justice, but were using her (as the man had used her) to bring about Jesus' downfall. In their eyes both the woman and Jesus were guilty, though of different offences. They thought they had him – as they thought they had her! She had been caught in the act. He was about to commit himself to words which would bring about his condemnation. But he took neither of the paths they had laid for him. He did not condemn, he did not excuse. He simply traced, seemingly idly, in the dust.

He allowed some time to elapse, lifted himself, and said those momentous words: 'Let anyone among you who is without sin be the first to throw a stone at her.' He then returned to writing in the dust. As a boy I saw a film in which one Pharisee after another looked over the shoulder of the bending Jesus and saw traced in the sand words like gluttony, avarice, lust, violence, cheating, hypocrisy, incest, and as they saw *their* word, slunk away in confusion.

Jesus did not resort to haggling over scripture texts using the subtleties of the Pharisees or Sadducees. He affirmed the

more profound pastoral theology of forgiveness. Condemnation only led to penalty and death, and if this is what
orthodoxy meant, then the ecclesiastics would say 'so be it'
because in their legalistic minds you have to pay the price that
orthodoxy demands. But Jesus understood it quite differently.
His was wisdom, not subtlety, and forgiveness affirmed a
theology which went to the very heart of God. The experience of forgiveness melted a sinful heart, transforming and
channelling the sinner's energies into the river of compassion,
and ultimately towards the ocean of Love.

But don't let us make this a case of situation ethics, which
excuses our sin. Jesus did not despise the Law, but revealed
another way in which the demands of law are fulfilled and
superseded by the better way of love. Jesus did not say,
'Neither do I condemn you, go in peace,' but 'Neither do I
condemn you. Go your way, and from now on do not sin
again.'

This pastoral text heartens me on this day in Lent, for one
day I shall stand before the Sinless One. What garment shall
I have to cover the shame of my naked sinfulness, hypocrisy
and guilt? Because of this scripture, which bears witness to
Jesus as the Man for Sinners, I can be clothed in the
righteousness of Christ, and know that his judgement is
tempered with mercy. He looked at her and asked about her
accusers. She looked at him and replied with wonder and
hope. He answered again, and his look, his words, his attitude
released a flood of gratitude and a new life. And that is just
what I need today.

PRAYER

Jesus, friend of sinners:
Sometimes we may be condemned unjustly, and rejected when
  we have not deserved it;
But sometimes we have hidden our sin, and cloaked our
  hypocrisies, projecting a respectable and acceptable image.
Forgive us for our dissembling, forgive us for joining in the
  condemnation of others when it makes us feel better about
  ourselves;
And in all things help us to refrain from the judgement of
  others, for only you know the human heart. Amen.

RESPONSE

This story is as much for church groups as for personal
evaluation. Does this story help you in your attitude to those
caught up in the different kinds of immoralities illustrated?
Are you quicker to condemn rather than comfort, to uphold
a strict theological orthodoxy, even if it treads upon the
sinner and behaves insensitively or even cruelly?

Reflect upon bringing together theological principle and
pastoral care in new ways, as Jesus did, neither disregarding
true justice nor condemning the sinner when he or she is
down.

Take a step today towards one who has been rejected in
church or society.

Lent 3: Tuesday

Unclean and Rejected

MARK 1:40-45; PSALM 38

A leper came to him begging him, and kneeling he said to him, 'If you choose, you can make me clean.' Moved with pity [anger], Jesus stretched out his hand and touched him, and said to him, 'I do choose. Be made clean!' Immediately the leprosy left him, and he was made clean.

Can you see this poor man, infected by that awful, contagious disease that attacks nerves and tissue, producing suppurating wounds which scare people away, and cause the victim to be cast out of ordinary society? Can you imagine the resulting attitude of self-loathing and fear which promises no hope or release, but leads only to begging from a leprosy settlement, and ends in a lonely and painful death? Not only had the leper lost his health and his place of self-respect in his Galilee village, but also those he loved – perhaps a wife and children he could never touch and kiss again. What trembling took hold of him as he observed the slow deterioration of his fellow lepers who had suffered for a longer period, serving as a cruel reflection of his own inevitable decline. Psalm 38 fits him exactly.

It was with a mingling of hope and fear that he ran up to Jesus one day, breaking the rules of quarantine, falling on his

THE WAY OF LOVE

knees and crying, 'If you choose, you can make me clean.' Then two amazing things took place. Anger and healing. In order to understand the anger you have to dig beneath the surface of the text.

The Greek differs in its readings. The best manuscripts have the verb *splagchnistheis*, which may be rendered 'being moved with passionate feeling' and can easily indicate pity or anger, or a mixture of both. A few inferior manuscripts have the verb *orgistheis*, which means 'being angry'. So it is not surprising that only the Revised English Bible translates 'Jesus was moved to anger . . .' while the other translations use words like 'pity' or 'compassion'. I have seen one paraphrase which renders 'moved by warm indignation'. Quite literally the Greek talks of a 'gut reaction'.

The truth is that Jesus was passionately angry with the disease that could reduce a human being to such a mass of putrifying sores and could wear him down to begging and cringing on his knees in such a desperate state. The passionate indignation which was Jesus' response to the poor man's plea was a mixture of anger against the situation which had laid the man so low, and a profound compassion that welled up within him in love for the sufferer.

'If you choose, you can make me clean,' cried the leper. 'I *do* choose,' responded Jesus, stretching out and touching him. 'Be clean!' And wonder of wonders – just like the flesh of Naaman, in the days of the prophet Elisha, who dipped himself in the river Jordan – the man's flesh became like that of a child again. It is like the chorus says:

100

He touched me! He touched me!
And oh, the joy that filled my soul;
Something happened, and I know
He touched me — and made me whole.

PRAYER

Lord Jesus Christ:
Your heart is filled with indignation against sin, your spirit
  is filled with compassion for all who suffer;
Look with pity upon all those who are afflicted in great
  pain, with terminal diseases and psychiatric illness.
Your will is wholeness and healing, so stretch out your hand,
  let your healing flow, let your power restore, and let your
  touch bring peace.
So shall your name be praised and your kingdom extended.
  Amen.

RESPONSE

Think of ways in which your righteous anger against injustice
may mingle with profound compassion for its victims, and
share with some friends ways in which positive good may
come from such thinking.

Groups
Think communally of people you know who may be suffering

from 'present-day leprosy' – with psychiatric problems, the HIV/AIDS virus, terminal cancer, Alzheimer's disease, or diseases of the muscular or central nervous system. Is there a healing group in your parish/neighbourhood, and what practical help is given to sufferers, and carers? Can you help? Ought you to?

Lent 3: Wednesday

Down Through the Roof

LUKE 5:17–26

'*Which is easier to say, "Your sins are forgiven you," or to say, "Stand up and walk"? But so that you may know that the Son of Man has authority on earth to forgive sins . . .' He said to the one who was paralysed, 'I say to you, stand up and take your bed and go to your home.' Immediately he stood up before them, took what he had been lying on, and went to his home, glorifying God.*

Amazement seized all of them, and they glorified God and were filled with awe, saying, 'We have seen strange things today.'

If Jesus is the Man for Sinners, then he is also the Divine Physician. This story reflects the ancient (and contemporary) view that we are a psychosomatic unity, that body and soul are inextricably bound together in one humanity. That means that anxiety, stress, guilt and an evil conscience can take their toll upon my physical well-being, and that joy, hope, compassion and love can also have an important influence on the physical organism and can promote good health. So states of mind can produce paralysis of the body. Jesus is therefore Physician and Saviour.

It has always been the emphasis of the Eastern churches to think of sin as a wounding or sickness, rather than press forensic and legalistic thinking regarding sin and atonement. When the injured victim was discovered by the Good Samaritan, he poured in oil and wine – oil symbolizing the soothing, healing Holy Spirit, and wine symbolizing the poured-out blood of Christ for cleansing. To think of sin as wounding sickness helps us to understand the image of God in humankind as marred and defaced, but not completely shattered and obliterated, and today's story illustrates this understanding.

The passage opens by telling us that the power of the Lord was with Jesus to heal. Jesus' power was sometimes conditioned by the faith and expectation present in his hearers (Matthew 13:58). So here we may assume that in spite of the presence of the Pharisees and professional legalists there was real faith among the people, and certainly great faith is kindled and communicated with the arrival of the four men carrying their paralysed friend on a pallet to present him to Jesus. These men have faith, ingenuity and persistence, for being unable to break through the crowd at the entrance, they climb up the outside steps to the roof of thatched straw, branches and dried clay. Nothing would stop them, so they break it up and lower their friend down to Jesus, who takes their holy boldness to heart and gets immediately to the root of the matter, saying, 'Friend, your sins are forgiven you.' This was the right way in, for although the man shared the faith of his friends, there was some connection between his physical state and his spiritual life.

The ecclesiastics were aghast at Jesus' authority – what they saw was presumption, and they were scared at the outshining of his power to heal. Forgiveness was the prerogative of God. They were more concerned with heresy hunting than with either forgiveness or healing, especially when their conception of God sustained the status quo, as organized and establishment religion has always done.

This did not deter the four friends, the paralytic man or Jesus, for faith was now flowing and expectations were high. Jesus shows how works follow faith as he uses the words which begin today's theme. The words of joyful command were spoken; the paralysed man stood to his feet, took up his pallet and walked boldly through the door, praising God as he went. Beautiful Greek words are used by Luke to register the result – *ekstasis* and *doxa* – ecstasy and glory! And filled with awe, the people cried, 'We have seen strange things today.'

PRAYER

Lord Jesus, Saviour and Healer:
We thank you that we can place our whole confidence in you
  for our ultimate salvation and healing; we thank you for
  the friends who surround us with their helping hands and
  living faith.
We pray for all those who oppose you in the name of status,
  establishment, religion, or because they are afraid.
Grant to all of us that we may be delivered from the paralysis
  of sin and fear, and let faith abound in the communities in
  which we live. Amen.

RESPONSE

Think of those times when you have been helped by the faith of others. Have you shown your gratitude by word and deed? Think of the ways in which you have been enabled to sustain others as the four friends carried their paralysed friend to Jesus. Do you realize the power of your faith in intercessory healing?

Groups

In what ways can you act together on behalf of the needy, through existing helping/healing agencies? Does a 'healing group' exist in your church/parish, meeting regularly simply to hold up the sick of the neighbourhood in words and silence, perhaps along the lines of the St Raphael healing groups?

Lent 3: Thursday

Friendship with Sinners

MATTHEW 9:9-13; PSALM 51:17

The Pharisees said to his disciples, 'Why does your teacher eat with tax collectors and sinners?'

But when he heard this he said, 'Those who are well have no need of a physician, but those who are sick. Go and learn what this means: "I desire mercy, not sacrifice." For I have come to call not the righteous but sinners.'

The sacrifice acceptable to God is a broken spirit; a broken and contrite heart, O God, you will not despise.

Controversy again! Why is it that religion makes some people so judgemental, so miserable, so legalistic, so fanatical, so bigoted, so violent? Why is it that so many wars around the world are fuelled by religion? And why is it that some people are better human beings *before* they become religious? Are these not reasons to shun religion? Well my answer would be 'yes' if by religion is meant the kind of religion which is evident in our scripture today. No religion is better than bad religion, because bad religion causes people to stone adulterers, burn witches, blast the enemy (who may be wearing the badge of Jew, Hindu, Christian, Sikh or whatever).

Jesus was not interested in making people religious, but leading them to a loving relationship with himself, and therefore with God. He offered forgiveness and healing to sin-sick souls as the basis of new life, opening up into a path of discipleship, compassion and mystical union with God. This means that once I let go my own self-righteous stance and admit myself a sinful, violent, self-centred individual, then open my life to the forgiveness and healing of Christ, a new principle of life is implanted. This is called being 'born again' of the Spirit of God.

But even this beautiful term 'born again' has been monopolized by a certain kind of Telly-evangelism and been brought into disrepute, so people are reluctant to be identified with it. I refuse to lose such a biblical and spiritual image. It is a great joy to say that I am a 'born again sinner', and that though I stumble and fall, my feet are on the way to becoming a more sympathetic and joyful human being. This is the way of forgiveness and non-violence, the way of dialogue and non-aggression, the way of compassion and openness.

The 'Crusade' kind of religion only leads to the adoption of even more military concepts and practices in the spreading of 'our religion'. This is why, once we think of 'our religious heritage', it becomes possible to think of defending it, imposing it, and then killing to do both. So 'Christian' nations can justify the sale of arms, employ a nuclear deterrent, and be prepared for the horror of using such weapons against other human beings. That is not the way of Christ.

Catholics and Protestants who maim and kill are not following the way of Christ; evangelicals and liberals who will make friends only with their own kind are not following the way of

Christ; those who marry Church and State in an uneasy mix of establishment religion for the sake of power or politics are not following the way of Christ.

I am very glad of my evangelical background, but there was sometimes a tendency (and this can be said of the catholic context too) to cultivate friendships to 'bring them to Christ'. This smacks not only of emotional blackmail, but made me suspicious of the whole enterprise, in a similar way that I would be careful of the approach of a person who I'd seen reading *How to Win Friends and Influence People*!

Well then, are there *any* Christians left on earth? Perhaps not. But the good news is that if we confess our need, our sins, our hypocrisies, and endeavour to live in the way of mutual forgiveness and humility, then at least our feet are on the way, our faces are toward the light, and our humanity is suffused with the humanity of Jesus.

Jesus is open to all people everywhere, and especially does he seek a place in gentleness and sympathy among sinners and outcasts. There are very real reasons why Matthew and his cronies are reckoned among the outcasts. First, they were thought unpatriotic, for this Matthew was probably engaged by the Roman representative who had bought the right to collect taxes in his area. Then, such tax collectors were given to extortion – the result being that not only was their money unacceptable as alms, but their evidence was unacceptable in a law court. They were outcast and despised.

Into such a situation Jesus comes with his offer of friendship, understanding and fellow-feeling – yet without condoning such malpractice. He loved the sinner but hated the sin. He came as friend and physician and not as judge and religionist. So sinners gathered round him, lepers dared to approach him, and the common people heard him gladly.

Jesus loved human beings, with a particular love for sinners and outcasts. His love was not for gain, for converts, for popularity, power or manipulation. He loved because he *was* love, and his *agape*-love was outgoing, generous and sacrificial. He extended his healing love as a true physician will seek out the sick and wounded — simply in order that they might be healed and restored to fullness of life.

PRAYER

Lord Jesus, lover of our fallen humanity:
Look upon your wounded world, upon the outcast and
despised, wounded and lonely.
Apply your healing art to the wounds of our sin and sickness,
restore true sense of humanity to those who have been cast
out of our society;
Restore us to fullness of life, and enable us, in our turn, to
befriend those who need your healing touch. Amen.

RESPONSE

Which groups constitute the outcasts in our society today? Are there any such in your neighbourhood, in your peer group, in your family? What about befriending an HIV/AIDS sufferer, helping a neighbour of a different racial and religious origin, or giving babysitting help to a one-parent family? Ask the Lord to open your heart to one or two areas of need, leading to genuine friendship and sympathetic concern.

Lent 3: Friday

Gentile, Woman and Nuisance

MATTHEW 15:21-28

She came and knelt before [Jesus] saying, 'Lord, help me.'

He answered, 'It is not fair to take the children's food and throw it to the dogs.'

She said, 'Yes, Lord, yet even the dogs eat the crumbs that fall from their masters' table.'

Then Jesus answered her, 'Woman, great is your faith! Let it be done for you as you wish.' And her daughter was healed instantly.

This is an amazing story, discomfiting to the reader if it is to be taken as it is written. The problem with some exegetes who don't like the pattern of the text is that they will suggest redaction and critical changes where there is no textual evidence. If the text is clear, then we must confront what is being said.

This is how it seems to me. Jesus had been involved in further bitter controversy with the religious authorities (vv 1-20), and had either been driven, or had made his own way, to the Gentile territory of Tyre and Sidon. It was increasingly clear that there was bitterness and bigotry, and a closed attitude on the part of religious Jewry. Jesus believed that Israel was called to be a light to the nations, and that his mission began with the lost sheep of the house of Israel. Here he was in a Gentile area, perhaps thinking through the meaning and method of his mission. Then a strange confrontation with Gentile faith took place which clarified the universality of his vocation.

The Canaanite woman came crying in an agony of maternal pain, using messianic language (she knew what she was about): 'Have mercy on me, Lord, Son of David; my daughter is tormented by a demon.' Jesus looked upon her and was silent. She kept on shouting. The disciples were irritated, for to them she was a Gentile, a woman and a nuisance. They were for sending her away, as they would have done with the children of Salem (Matthew 19:13).

It is difficult to know the nuance or the purpose of the words Jesus eventually spoke: 'I was sent only to the lost sheep of the house of Israel.' Of course he *was* Israel personified, the Servant of the Lord sent to Israel as the elect nation. But he nowhere else uses the exclusive word 'only'.

She fell before him in further appeal, and he provoked her still further: 'It is not fair to take the children's food and throw it to the dogs.' Perhaps he was thinking ironically that he himself had been casting pearls before swine in his previous dispute with the unbelieving Jewish authorities. Anyway, these words sparked in the woman a lively, discerning, subtle response, full of faith and yet humble in its expectancy.

Jesus was splendidly surprised, as with the Gentile centurion (Matthew 8:10), and he poured grace upon her,

113

and healing upon her daughter. Perhaps in this moment he felt that inward witness of the Spirit that God's grace is universal, fathomless and completely benevolent, and he was its channel and instru-ment. Jesus opened his mind, his heart, his love to her, confirming the universality of his mission in the immediacy of his response: 'And her daughter was healed instantly.'

PRAYER

Lord Jesus, reconciling Saviour:

Many of my non-Christian friends cannot believe that such universal compassion as yours exists, or they cannot believe it embraces them;

Many of my Christian friends somehow do not give the impression of such free and boundless love — and perhaps I am among them.

Grant us such a change of heart, such a transformation of attitude, such a kindling of sympathy and divine joy that its radiance and heat shall warm all those around, and enable them to draw closer to the fire from the bleak coldness of an indiffernt world. Amen.

RESPONSE

Do you find, in Jesus, an unusual exclusivist attitude to this woman? If so, what do you think are the reasons? Was he intending from the outset to heal her daughter, and is there an element of 'teasing out' her faith? How do you account for the evident surprise on his part?

Groups

How universal was Jesus' mission? Did he know from his baptism, or was there a gradual unfolding in exploration — and was this incident one of divine disclosure to him?

What about *your* understanding of your, or the Church's, mission? People of other faiths make their appeal to God — does he hear them? Even if they are not in 'the Church' could they be included in 'the kingdom'?

Lent 3: Saturday

Remember Me!

LUKE 23:32-43

*O*ne *of the criminals who were hanged there kept deriding him and saying, 'Are you not the Messiah? Save yourself and us!'*

But the other rebuked him, saying, 'Do you not fear God, since you are under the same sentence of condemnation? And we indeed have been condemned justly, for we are getting what we deserve for our deeds, but this man has done nothing wrong.' Then he said, 'Jesus, remember me when you come into your kingdom.'

He replied, 'Truly I tell you, today you will be with me in paradise.'

There were three crosses: two sinners and the Saviour. 'One sinner was saved that none need despair,' said old Bishop Ryle, 'but only one, that none should presume.' The difference was between a penitent and an obdurate sinner. Both were malefactors, both had been caught, tried, condemned and cast outside the city wall to be crucified in the place of a skull. One of them cursed in life and cursed in death, and even showed a trace of cunning in his last hours: 'Are you not the Messiah?

Save yourself and us!' But the other, for reasons that are hidden from us, believed that this lacerated, exhausted, bleeding, crucified man was somehow crowned, though with thorns; and upon a throne, though it was a cross – regal in his dying and with the whole kingdom of heaven before him.

A poem I once read suggested that this penitent man, one of a band of marauders, had once crept upon Jesus when he was speaking with the people in the hills above Galilee. He hid himself among the boulders, watching and listening, until, at one moment, Jesus turned his head and caught his gaze, in mid-sentence: 'Come to me, all you that are weary and are carrying heavy burdens, and I will give you rest.' (Matthew 11:28) All through the following months, in the solitude of his own soul and through the emptiness of his outcast and unsatisfying life, those words had haunted him, as had the eyes that had held him for those moments.

Now at last, when the weariness was dimming his eyes in his dying, and the burden of his body, his conscience and of his sins was pressing down upon him, he turned his head painfully and looked upon the crucified King of Glory, making a dying confession of faith and hope: 'Jesus, remember me when you come into your kingdom.' He was met by that same gaze, those sorrowful eyes, that loving heart, and it called him again.

As he waited he heard the words that brought peace and rest to him in that moment, words heavy with the promise of the kingdom, not in some far-off day of judgement, but today, just beyond the valley of the shadow from which the light was already beginning to shine: 'Truly I tell you, today you will be with me in paradise.'

As these days of Lent progress we shall be drawing nearer

to the cross and the whole sorrow of Calvary. But today we look at the cross of penitence, where anguish was being transformed into dying glory, where midnight was moving into an undreamed-of dawn.

What about your death and mine? When it will be, or where it will be is mercifully hidden from us, but *that* it will be is most certain. We need not despair, but we must not presume. Whatever sins and burdens we bear, however deceitful and shabby our lives, whatever relationships we have betrayed, and however many hopes and aspirations have failed – here today, as our Lord's face is turned towards us, as he holds our gaze and calls us deep within our souls, we can turn to him, and murmur quietly in penitence and faith: 'Jesus, remember me.'

This can happen at the deathbed of a notorious sinner, but grace cannot be presumed upon. It can only truly happen where there is a spirit of longing, of need, of repentance. But where such a moment occurs, there is the beginning of a pilgrimage to the kingdom, for that kingdom is born in the soul, and yet shines from the other side of the valley of the shadow of death.

PRAYER

Lord Jesus, friend of the crucified:
What was it that caused the dying thief to discern your glory?
Was it the writing above your head on the cross? Was it
some previous encounter, some miracle witnessed or some
parable about God's love for the sinner?

Whatever it was, when the hour for dying came, you were
there. Be there for me in the hour of my dying.

May I take all the opportunities for grace, faith and love
which are offered me today, so that I shall hear your
words: 'Truly I tell you, today you will be with me in
paradise.' Amen.

RESPONSE

There is the possibility of repentance and new life for anyone, whatever they may have done. Will you undertake to pray for those who have been condemned, convicted, imprisoned as perpetrators of evil? Will you write to one, visit him or her? Will you seek out their relatives and inform yourself of the work of prison chaplains and prison Christian fellowships?

LENT 4
Jesus, Man of Divinity

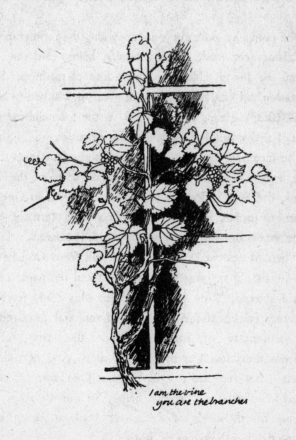

I am the vine
you are the branches

The 'I am' Sayings of Jesus

'BEFORE ABRAHAM WAS, I AM' (JOHN 8:58)

The evangelist portrays Jesus as making the most stupendous claim ever made by any human being, and one which incited the Jewish elders to accuse him of madness, demon-possession and blasphemy! He, being a man, claimed to be God (John 10:33). Here, in John 8:58, is the fountainhead of the great 'I am' sayings of Jesus: 'Before Abraham was, I am.'

The Incarnate Logos is speaking. The human Jesus did not exist before Bethlehem, but John speaks to us of the eternal Logos, the Second Person of the divine Three-in-One, who became incarnate in Jesus – yet who was, eternally. 'There never was a time when he was not.' *St Athanasius.*

When Moses received the divine call from God he asked who he should say sent him, and he asked the name of God. God answered, 'I AM WHO I AM.' (Exodus 3:14) Jewish and Christian commentators have wondered and laboured over the profundity of that name, of that text, of that confrontation, for it is as deep as deity. And here Jesus is claiming that very name – the timeless One, from all eternity – and manifested in a human being, for our salvation.

This fourth week of Lent, we look at seven of the Johannine 'I am' sayings of Jesus.

Lent 4: Sunday

'I am the Bread of Life'

JOHN 6:1-15, 25-66

'*Your ancestors ate the manna in the wilderness, and they died. This is the bread that comes down from heaven, so that one may eat of it and not die. I am the living bread that came down from heaven. Whoever eats of this bread will live for ever; and the bread that I will give for the life of the world is my flesh.*'

I regularly bake my own bread in my hermitage, and my writing about it has caused others to take delight in making their own bread (*Forty Days and Forty Nights*, p. 58). I use my own recipe for making bread for the eucharist, for it does seem that to use real bread and not rice paper for holy communion is what our Lord intended. I also pray as I make my bread. Our Lord's use of the eating of bread offers a very basic and practical way of making me understand that I need to feed upon him at every level of my being — in my common meals, at holy communion, in listening to his word in scrip-ture, and in the deep places of prayer and loving service. Only as I feed upon Christ himself will my soul be sustained and will I be able to communicate his life and love to others.

In today's scripture we are told the story of Jesus multiplying bread and feeding the crowd, with the sad result that
many of them followed him simply on that material level, so
that he had to say, 'You are looking for me . . . because you
ate your fill of the loaves. Do not work for the food that
perishes but for the food that endures for eternal life, which
the Son of Man will give you.' (vv 26-27) Throughout this
chapter Jesus is saying, 'I am the bread of life', not merely,
'I give the bread of life'. It is himself, alone, who can satisfy
the hungry soul. The people acknowledged their physical
hunger, but were unable to see in Jesus the sustenance for
heart and spirit that only he could supply.

As the chapter goes on, Jesus not only diagnoses the human
condition of intellectual, moral, emotional and spiritual hunger,
but makes the first of our 'I am' claims to be the bread of life,
which would satisfy the spiritual and eternal hunger of his
hearers. They began to misunderstand, argue among themselves, and then fall into violent controversy and rejection of
Jesus. He was a local boy of parents that they knew, and they
could not therefore accept such astounding messianic claims.
Then they fell into doctrinal and literalist disputes about eating
his flesh and drinking his blood, and even some disciples were
scandalized and turned from him (v 66).

There is eucharistic teaching here, and John understands
that the bread and wine of the eucharist is the body and blood
of the Lord, but he has no literalist dogma to expound.
Indeed he records Jesus as saying 'It is the Spirit that gives
life; the flesh is useless. The words that I have spoken to you
are spirit and life.' (v 63) When Thomas Aquinas used the
substance philosophy to illustrate the presence of Christ in the

sacrament, he was endeavouring to illuminate the reality of that presence and not putting up dogmatic fences to keep people away.

Jesus, the Bread of Life, is offered to any who will turn to him in living faith, and he mediates his living, loving presence through word and sacrament. Jesus, the Bread of Life, can feed Christians who come to the altar for holy communion, and can also truly feed members of the Salvation Army or Quakers who have no sacrament of the eucharist but who gather savingly around the word of God. The important thing is to feed upon Jesus himself, to encounter him in his risen life, and to allow his word access into the hungry and yearning human soul. As the eleventh-century Latin hymn has it:

We taste Thee, O Thou living Bread,
   And long to feast upon Thee still;
We drink of Thee, the Fountainhead,
   And thirst our souls from Thee to fill.

PRAYER

Lord Jesus, Bread of Life:
We come to you famished and unsatisfied after tasting the
   vanities and pleasures of the world, after wasting the
   energy of mind and spirit on temporal pleasures and sins
   that mock us in our deepest need.

We come to you, who alone can satisfy our eternal hunger,
and pray, Lord, give us this bread for evermore. Amen.

RESPONSE

Why not bake a simple recipe of bread (even if it is the first time), then write out the hymn 'Jesus, Thou joy of loving hearts', and give both bread and hymn to a friend or neighbour as a gift? You may prove the significance of the words: 'Send out your bread upon the waters, for after many days you will get it back.' (Ecclesiastes 11:1)

Lent 4: Monday

'I am the Light of the World'

ISAIAH 9:1-2; JOHN 9:1-41

The people who walked in darkness have seen a great light; those who lived in a land of deep darkness — on them the light has shined.

They kept asking him, 'How were your eyes opened?' He answered, 'The man called Jesus made mud, spread it on my eyes, and said to me, "Go to Siloam and wash." Then I went and washed and received my sight.'

If this claim was not so familiar, it would blow our minds! 'I am the light of the world. Whoever follows me will never walk in darkness but will have the light of life.' There has been, and could be, no other like it, for it is without limit of space, time, sphere or power, and wholly belongs to truth and love.

There have been many religious teachers, and among them much truth, insight, compassion and understanding of the wonder of God has been discerned and shared. I am thinking of the great ones, like the Buddha, Ramakrishna, Mohammed, Guru Nanak, and especially the root tradition of Judaism. But there has been no claim like this, and there is no one like

Jesus. They are lights and illuminations that shine in the world, but only Christ is the Light. They share great teaching, but he is the Light itself. Far from denigrating their influence and truth, at best they are reflections of the true Light which enlightens everyone who comes into the world (John 1:4).

This means that if we are truly following the light of Jesus, we shall be open to his light wherever it may be found. Certainly, I have found Jesus in the teaching of the Buddha, in the beauty of the life of Ramakrishna, in the devotion of the Sufi mystics, and in the witness of the Sikh Guru Nanak. Yet they are but reflections of God incarnate in Jesus Christ, and his reflection I find in everything good and true and beautiful in all the world.

This is not merely a concept or image, for Jesus as the Light illuminates the page of scripture, and shines in human experience in the story of the man born blind. Consider the areas of the man's life which were brought to life by the divine illumination:

Physical sight. Blind from birth, there was the awareness of physical deprivation, a kindling of hope in meeting Jesus, a venture of faith in obedience to Jesus' word, with the resulting miracle of physical sight.

Intellectual quickening. Notice the progression of his mental awareness: 'Jesus made mud . . . spread it . . . sent me to wash' (v 11). 'He is a prophet' (v 17). 'Not a sinner . . . a sight giver, and therefore from God' (vv 30–33).

Spiritual vision. The light of Christ, illuminating his body, mind and spirit, resulted in the growing experience which led to the confession: 'One thing I do know, that though I was blind, now I see' (v 25), and 'Lord, I believe' (v 38). The result of all this was that he worshipped Jesus as Lord and Messiah.

Therefore, if Jesus becomes the light of our lives we shall not walk in darkness, but continually experience his radiance in our lives and relationships. It will mean that my life is open and honest before God and before my fellow creatures. I say 'creatures' for when the Buddhist tradition speaks of the sacredness of life and compassion for 'all sentient beings' it includes the animal world as well. More and more we are becoming aware of the light of Christ shining upon our human relationships, and upon our use, abuse and care of the animal and ecological order.

If the light of Christ shines within my personal and communal life, I should be a better, humbler, more compassionate, honest and open human being, working towards the alleviation of all suffering and the illuminating of all the dark places of our world.

PRAYER

Lord Jesus, Light of the World:
Grant that living in your light I may feel the
responsibility of sharing its radiance and warmth.
Enable me to recognize the remaining darkness in my
thinking, living and influence.

THE WAY OF LOVE

Grant that your suffusing glory may shine wherever human beings relate to each other in personal and international affairs, for you are the Light of the World. Amen.

RESPONSE

Have you considered the light of Christ in the lives and teachings of other faiths? Gandhi said that his favourite Christian hymn was 'When I survey the wondrous cross'. Have you discovered a sense of God in the writings of other faiths? If you have a friend or neighbour of another faith, ask him or her to share with you something of their own inspirational texts, and perhaps they may like to ask the same of you.

130

Lent 4: Tuesday

'I am the Door'

JOHN 10:7–10

Jesus said, ' . . . I am the gate [door] for the sheep. All who came before me were thieves and bandits; but the sheep did not listen to them. I am the gate. Whoever enters by me will be saved, and will come in and go out and find pasture. The thief comes only to steal and kill and destroy. I came that they may have life, and have it abundantly.'

However many doors of opportunity I may have missed, whatever doors of hope have been shut in my face, whatever doors of exciting relationships and personal ambition have been closed against me, there is one door that once opened to me, and is forever open. That door is Christ. In which way is Jesus the Door, and what does this claim mean?

Firstly, he is the door to the Father's heart. I heard, believed, and understood the simple language of Jesus in his humanity, with the invitation to enter into a loving trust in him as my Saviour. I found myself, through his humanity, entering into the divinity of the divine Love, the divine Mercy, the divine Godhead, with all the mysteries of participation in the life of God.

Secondly, he is the door into the safety of the sheepfold. The hillside sheepfold was a simple wall enclosure with just an opening for entrance. At night the shepherd himself lay down across the opening, keeping the sheep securely *in*, and the wolves completely *out!* There are dark nights when Jesus assures me of this kind of protection against demon powers and marauding evil, for he, himself, is my protection and security.

Thirdly, he is the door to sustaining pastures, for the fold is not a prison, and I am encouraged to go 'in and out' in the glorious freedom of the flock of God. The pastures broaden out into all the goodness and truth of our world, and all the sustaining power of true religion and spiritual relationships.

Fourthly, he is the door into the one, eternal fold. That fold is not an exclusive church or demonination, but the breadth of the kingdom of God, which is the dominion of love and compassion.

The 'thieves and bandits' who came before him, that Jesus refers to, are not the previous prophets up to John the Baptist, of course. They are those pseudo-messiahs who, in the name of patriotism and religion, promised the messianic, golden age, but by methods of violence, insurrection and bloodshed. In Jesus' teaching, if the means are evil, then the end must be evil.

There may be many other varieties and breeds of sheep which he will at last bring home (John 10:16), and the mind boggles at the immensity of this thought, but there is only one Door, and one Shepherd – and his name is Jesus.

PRAYER

Lord Jesus, Door to the Father's heart:
Let me truly cross over the threshold, through your sacred
  humanity;
Let me enter ever more deeply into the life of God in the
  depths of the Spirit;
Enable me to leave behind all the baggage of sin and self,
  and to take that step of faith, through the door, and into
  the new dimension of love. Amen.

RESPONSE

The Response today is relevant to the individual reader and to group participation.

Write down names on the doors which you *could* have gone through, but did not; then some doors which you *would* have gone through but were prevented; then some doors which you *should* have gone through, but you were afraid. What about the doors which you found locked and barred against you? And those doors which you realized later that you had missed and others had entered?

Has it turned out well? Can you see God's hindering grace, prompting grace, and the grace which led you to Christ the Door?

Could you hold open a door of opportunity and hope for someone at present in your life? Do it – with prayer and joy.

Lent 4: Wednesday

'I am the Good Shepherd'

JOHN 10:11-18, 27-30

I am the good shepherd. I know my own, and my own know me, just as the Father knows me and I know the Father. And I lay down my life for the sheep. I have other sheep that do not belong to this fold. I must bring them also, and they will listen to my voice. So there will be one flock, one shepherd.'

Today's scripture passage reveals in how great a danger the sheep would be were it not for the good and true shepherd. Quite apart from wild animals, there is the robber who would fleece or even kill the sheep for his own benefit. Then there is the hireling who is simply doing the job for the money, and when the testing time comes and danger threatens he runs off, for he has care for his own skin and not for the safety of the sheep.

In contrast, we have the Good Shepherd. The descriptive word means *good*, not in the sense of moral rectitude, but of attractiveness, of beauty. This is the shepherd who was born to the task, has a vocation to shepherding, holds the sheep in trust for the Owner, and for love of them will sacrifice his own life. Between shepherd and sheep is the mutual understanding of love, so that if they are mixed with other sheep in an overnight fold, or on the hillside, and he calls, then they answer him.

If one of them should stray and be lost down some rocky crevice, he will seek for that one until he finds it (Luke 15:3-7). That childhood picture in my illustrated Bible is before me now — a shepherd stretches over a precariously rocky crevice, taking hold of the frightened and trembling lamb on the lower ledge with his crook. And implicit in the picture is the resulting reunion, embrace and rejoicing.

The joy of Jesus as the Good Shepherd is to love and sustain the sheep of God, to lead them to pasture and water from morning to evening, and to secure them in the fold of his love at night, himself lying between them and the bear or lion who would attack the flock. As David the shepherd said to King Saul, 'Your servant used to keep sheep for his father; and whenever a lion or a bear came, and took a lamb from the flock, I went after it and struck it down, rescuing the lamb from its mouth.' (1 Samuel 17:34–35)

The love of the Good Shepherd is supremely revealed in his sacrificial surrender of his life for the sheep, but that love is also manifested in the tender communion between them — he speaks to them each by its own name, and they recognize such personal tenderness. As one of his sheep, I recognize that communion and tenderness he shows toward me, so that as I meditate upon Jesus, the Good, the Beautiful Shepherd, I sing quietly:

Let the beauty of Jesus be seen in me,
All his wondrous compassion and purity;

Holy Spirit divine, all my nature refine,
Till the beauty of Jesus is seen in me.

I love the old King James' Bible with which I was brought up, but there is a mistranslation in verse 16 where it says 'there will be one *fold*, one shepherd', when it should say, 'one *flock*, one shepherd'. Thinking that *my* fold, my denomination, my church, is the only one leads us to exclusivism and even bigotry and fanaticism. There is only one Church, with a capital 'C', but that is the Church of God in which all the 'folds' or communions have their part – the Methodists, the Roman Catholics, the Quakers, the Orthodox, the Baptists, the Pentecostals, the Lutherans, the Anglicans – indeed all those who confess Jesus Christ as Lord. Even that Church is part of the wider kingdom.

As for the kingdom of God, well only God knows the length and breadth, the depth and height – it is the measure of love. The Good Shepherd will bring home all the 'other sheep', and will offer them all to the Father, when God will be all in all. (1 Corinthians 15:28)

PRAYER

Lord Jesus, Shepherd of the sheep:
You are the Good Shepherd who laid down his life for us; you
are the Great Shepherd who was raised from the dead; you
are the Chief Shepherd who will appear in glory to bring
home all your redeemed flock.
Grant that we may hear your voice and follow in loving

obedience, so that from many folds we may comprise one
flock, under one Shepherd. Amen.

RESPONSE

Half-way through writing this meditation, Alistair came to see
me. He is staying at the monastery on retreat before his ordina-
tion on Sunday. He will serve as a non-stipendiary priest. He
is a village doctor near Hereford, and he also has a smallholding
with sheep, horses, geese and hens. We talked about
shepherding, pastoral care, holistic medicine, theology, and
Jesus as the Good Shepherd.

His response to Jesus calling him by name is clear – what is
yours?

Lent 4: Thursday

'I am the Resurrection and the Life'

JOHN 11:1-37

Jesus said to [Martha], 'Your brother will rise again.'

Martha said to him, 'I know that he will rise again in the resurrection on the last day.'

Jesus said to her, 'I am the resurrection and the life. Those who believe in me, even though they die, will live; and everyone who lives and believes in me will never die. Do you believe this?'

She said to him, 'Yes, Lord, I believe that you are the Messiah, the Son of God, the one coming into the world.'

With our scripture passage before us, there are three profound lessons for us to learn on our knees today.

Firstly, Jesus seems to have failed to answer an urgent call. 'Lord, he whom you love is ill' was the cry from the sisters of Lazarus. Jesus said something that the disciples misunderstood and remained two more days in that place. This is sometimes how it seems to us. We have been like Mary and Martha, anxiously glancing along the road while the life of Lazarus burned low, approaching death. Still he did not come, and the light flickered — and went out. In need . . . in extreme sickness . . . in bereavement — and still he did not come. He gives no sign, he seems not to respond, he does not come.

Secondly, after seeming to assure the disciples that Lazarus will not die, he points the disciples in the direction of risk, towards the shadow of the cross. Then when they confess their fears and perplexity, he faces them with the truth of Lazarus' death, and the long shadow of Calvary grows in their hearts.

It is at this time that Jesus is exploring his own interior Gethsemane, offering himself to the Father on Lazarus' behalf, and understanding the way forward. Because he has set his face towards his Father's will, and his life is in the hands of God, nothing can fail, though it lead through the way of sorrow and darkness. The fact that Jesus 'knew' and set his face resolutely towards Jerusalem does not lessen the anguish, the sorrow, the sin-bearing — indeed it intensifies it in his soul — for our sakes. This is what the disciples will realize after the whole event, and this is what is set out in John's gospel.

Thirdly, Jesus comes at last, and evokes such trust and yearning in the sisters that the power of death is broken for them. They experience Jesus to be the resurrection and the life.

First Martha comes. In spite of her grief she goes out to meet Jesus and speaks of his power. If only he had been there . . . Then she speaks such strange words that she hardly knows what she is saying: 'even now I know that God will give you whatever you ask of him.' Jesus speaks words of consolation from the depth of Jewish faith, and Martha replies with an affirmation born of trust: 'I know that he will rise again in the resurrection on the last day.'

Jesus met teaching with teaching, and then suddenly presented her with the stupendous words which have wakened hope in the hearts of multitudes down the ages: 'I am the resurrection and the life. Those who believe in me even though they die, will live; and everyone who lives and believes in me will never die.' Then Martha stammered out her confession of Jesus as the Son of God, saw the glory in his face, and it dawned on her that something amazing was about to happen.

She ran off to get her sister. Mary came to Jesus quickly, and falling down before him, cried out, 'If only . . .' and opened her heart in sorrow and weeping. Jesus did not impart any theological teaching, but simply allowed the grief and sorrow of the whole bereaved world to move him to the depths of his being through Mary's tears. And he mingled her tears with his own.

All this took place before the mighty act of the raising of Lazarus. Jesus shared the consolation of the truth of life beyond the grave for all believers, and then he showed himself to be the hope and basis of risen life here and now. For unless Jesus rises within the dark tomb of our yearning hearts, we cannot hope for life in Christ within the communion of saints in the life to come.

This Lazarus story not only transforms our present existence and links our life with the life of Jesus now, but stirs up personal and corporate hope in the larger life in Christ which is cosmic in its scope, and which embraces the whole of creation:

With mercy and with judgement
  My web of time he wove,
And aye the dews of sorrow
  Were lustred by his love:
I'll bless the hand that guided,
  I'll bless the heart that planned,
When throned where glory dwelleth
  In Immanuel's land.

PRAYER

Lord Jesus, Prince of Life:
There are times when I cannot discern your light in the
  darkness, and when you seem not to hear my cry;
There are times when I have to learn hard lessons in
  loneliness, sickness and bereavement;
Yet always I learn that it is not my feeling of your loving
  presence that matters, but the fact of it, for I need to
  learn to walk by faith and not by sight.
Come to me today and show yourself to be my life; be near
  me in the hour of my dying, and take me to your heart
  of love.
Jesus, my resurrection, and my life. Amen.

RESPONSE

In her book *On Death and Dying*, Elisabeth Kübler-Ross out-
lines a fivefold pattern in the process from terminal diagnosis

to dying. They are denial, anger, bargaining, depression and acceptance.

Think about these now, and find out more about this whole area of dying, so that you will be strengthened to face your own finitude and mortality, and be enabled to be with others as they discover theirs. For these are milestones that Jesus makes real to us on our journey with him.

Lent 4: Friday

'I am the Way, the Truth and the Life'

JOHN 14:1-14

Thomas said to him, 'Lord, we do not know where you are going. How can we know the way?' Jesus said to him, 'I am the way, and the truth, and the life. No one comes to the Father except through me. If you know me, you will know my Father also. From now on, you do know him and have seen him.'

Poor Thomas has been dubbed 'the doubter'. Yet that very quality of honest yearning caused Jesus to use the amazing words of our theme today, and later caused Thomas to cry in abandoned adoration, 'My Lord and my God.'

Jesus was going to the Father, and the way was the way of the cross. He had told the disciples this in so many ways, but they were unable to perceive, to understand, because this was truth in the divine sense. 'Lord, we do not know where you are going,' said Thomas, 'How can we know the way?' Then Jesus opened his heart:

'*I am the Way*' All the Old Testament wisdom and prophecy concerning the way is summed up in the beautiful picture of the 'Holy Way' in Isaiah 35:8-10. He pictures the paradise of God, blossoming with the flowers and trees of God's glory;

where all sickness, pain and sorrow are removed; where fertility and living waters abound; where no wild creatures or catastrophes can invade; where the redeemed and ransomed of the Lord shall walk, singing with joy and gladness; and where sorrow and sighing shall flee away. The Old Testament is struggling here to show that to dwell in God, in the justice, wisdom and love of God, is the 'way to be', the 'way to live'; and the fulfilling of the law of wisdom is the first tottering step to such a goal.

There was only One who could fulfil this wisdom and, incarnate in himself, the perfection of this Way. He did not come to show us how to do it, to teach us more intensely, or to exemplify it more perfectly. He came to incarnate his love, his very self in us. That is why he said, 'I am the Way.'

We are not incorporated into the Way by following the life or counsel of the holiest of the apostles, nor by imitating the life of that amazing Christian, St Francis of Assisi. The only way is by surrendering our lives to the indwelling of the Person of Jesus, for he is the Way to the Father, and in him we are born again.

For Jesus, the way to the Father was via the cross, and this is told out in the experience of all those who follow him. As Paul said, 'I have been crucified with Christ, and it is no longer I who live, but it is Christ who lives in me.' (Galatians 2:19-20)

'*I am the Truth*' Jesus does not teach a set of propositions, a catechism of dogma, or even a practical set of ethics. That is not to say that there is no instruction, teaching, doctrine, and manner of life — but these are secondary. It is only by opening our minds, hearts and lives to Jesus himself that we discern and understand the truth. If he is the centre of our lives, and if his love and compassion are incarnated in us, then we shall understand the teaching (John 7:17), and be able to live out the Christ life. Jesus did not say 'I *teach* the Truth', or even 'I *exemplify* the Truth', but 'I *am* the Truth'. And the Truth shall make us free.

'*I am the Life*' It was clear to anyone who was forgiven or healed by Jesus that he was the life-giving source of their new vitality. The poor woman whose life was barren and dried up by a chronic haemorrhage simply touched him who was the Life, and the surging, dynamic energy of new life coursed through her veins: 'she felt in her body that she was healed' (Mark 5:29).

The disciples on the dark side of Easter could only listen, observe, strive to obey, endeavour to trust. Yet they did not understand, and all of them deserted Jesus at the last (Mark 14:50). But on the glory side of Easter the risen Christ appeared to them, the Holy Spirit descended upon them, and they entered into the true mystical life of the indwelling Christ.

Thus he became, in living experience, the Way to the Father, the Truth which is the basis of all reality, and the Life which fully and abundantly spreads to all with whom it comes into contact.

PRAYER

Lord Jesus, image of the Father:
Without the Way there is no going, without the Truth there is
no knowing, without the Life there is no living;

*Come then and dwell deep within our hearts, that we may
walk joyfully, learn obediently and live lovingly, so that
the world may see that your life shines through our lives
today.* Amen.

RESPONSE

Today we learn that the secret of the Christian life is the
mystical indwelling of Christ himself in the believer and in the
Church. The roots of such a spirituality can only be sustained
by the life of prayer, both personal and sacramental. Are you
being sustained at these levels in your own spiritual life?

Groups

Is there teaching and practice of contemplative prayer in your
church and parish? Methods of meditation and teaching on the
life of prayer should be part of every parish. Perhaps your
group should pioneer the way if there is a 'contemplative gap'
in your fellowship.

Lent 4: Saturday

'I am the True Vine'

JOHN 15:1-11

'*I am the true vine, and my Father is the vinegrower. He removes every branch in me that bears no fruit. Every branch that bears fruit he prunes to make it bear more fruit. You have already been cleansed by the word that I have spoken to you. Abide in me as I abide in you. Just as the branch cannot bear fruit by itself unless it abides in the vine, neither can you unless you abide in me. I am the vine, you are the branches. Those who abide in me and I in them bear much fruit, because apart from me you can do nothing.*'

The vine was a beautiful symbol of God's ancient people throughout the Old Testament, depicted in Isaiah, Jeremiah, Ezekiel, Hosea and the Psalms. Yet the context is usually that Israel has become a degenerate vine, that it is barren, or that it yielded wild and useless grapes (Isaiah 5:1-7). The love song concerning the vineyard which had been cultivated, tended, nurtured, turns into a dirge and a song of judgement as the Lord bewails the barrenness of Israel.

The vinegrower is the Father, and the vine is the Son, planted into the earth by the incarnation. The branches are the members of Christ, grown or grafted into the living vine, with the nutritious sap flowing through the whole vine, promoting growth and fruitfulness. Throughout the seasons the vinegrower tends the vine, sometimes pruning it gently, other times seemingly cruelly in order that it may bring forth fruit . . . more fruit . . . much fruit (vv 4-5).

This is the most telling organic illustration of the believer's mystical union with Christ, and the Church's unity in the true vine. The fruit is not produced by separate branches, apart from the parent vine, for as Jesus says, 'apart from me you can do nothing.' The vine and the branches in the teaching of Jesus are the counterpart of Paul's organic model of the body and its members. Christ is the vine bearing its branches; Christ is the Head of the body.

The secret is 'abiding' or resting in Christ. There is a certain passivity about it, for we are not saved or sanctified by exertion, but by allowing the mystical life of Christ to flow through us as the sap courses through the branches of the vine. But this passivity is not inactivity. It is rather the nurturing of a mystical and contemplative spirit of prayer, sacrament and scripture in the loving presence of God, which results in fruit-bearing in the world. It is natural, seasonal, not forced or mechanistic, and certainly is not a result of frenetic activity which often marks the modern Christian and the organized Church.

The seasons also dictate the growth. In our lives we must learn that we cannot always live in the springtime of the rising of new sap, or the summer of growth and formation; we cannot always live in the autumn of rich fruit-bearing, or in the winter of rest and seeming deadness. Each of these seasons has its place, and all are interdependent and necessary.

Then there is the pruning. This is necessary but painful. The vine is cultivated in order that it may bring forth abundant fruit, and that is only possible as the luxuriant growth is pruned back. It is a discipline, an ascesis which is part of all creative life and talent – as much for the musician, the artist, the athlete, as for the vinegrower.

There are many branches in the one vine. I have been exploring the hermit life for the last five years. There has been much purging and pruning involved, and, I hope, some fruit-bearing. But I am also part of the Franciscan family, and we are not a hermit Order! My brothers and sisters are fruit-bearing branches in the areas of evangelism, teaching, retreats, peace and justice, care for the poor and deprived, as well as the life of prayer and worship.

The vine produces grapes, and the grapes are crushed to produce wine. Among the lovely eucharistic hymns to Christ are the following stanzas by John S. B. Monsell:

Thou bruised and broken Bread,
   My lifelong wants supply;
As living souls are fed
   O feed me, or I die.

Thou true life-giving Vine,
   Let me Thy sweetness prove,
Renew my life with Thine,
   Refresh my soul with love.

PRAYER

Lord Jesus, Vine of Heaven:
I long to abide in you, a living and fruit-bearing branch of
the true vine.
Grant that I may learn from the pruning experiences of my
life, and discern the value of the changing seasons, so
that when the renewing sap flows through the branches of
the vine, I may rejoice and bear fruit for the joy of the
world. Amen.

RESPONSE

Look up a good devotional commentary on this passage.
Apply the lessons of the vine in the Old and New Testaments
to your life and the life of the Church.

Then discuss with your friends/group ways in which
pruning may take place, and the kind of fruit which may
glorify God in your life and parish.

LENT 5

Jesus, Man of Sorrows

When I am lifted up
I will draw all people to myself

Lent 5: Sunday

The Suffering Servant

ISAIAH 53; ACTS 8:26-40

He was despised and rejected by others; a man of suffering and acquainted with infirmity; and as one from whom others hide their faces he was despised and we held him of no account. Surely he has borne our infirmities and carried our diseases; yet we accounted him stricken, struck down by God and afflicted. But he was wounded for our transgressions, crushed for our iniquities; upon him was the punishment that made us whole, and by his bruises we are healed.

The eunuch asked Philip, 'About whom, may I ask you, does the prophet say this? About himself or about someone else?' Then Philip began to speak, and starting with this scripture, he proclaimed to him the good news about Jesus.

It is amazing how a passage of scripture can be suffused with profound beauty and meaning by the way it is read or sung. I was only about thirteen when I first heard Handel's setting of 'He was despised . . .' from *Messiah*, but I was profoundly moved by its lovely pathos, its melancholy, its power to lift the listener to a form of contemplative prayer on the suffering of Christ.

The early Church quickly saw the intimate relationship between the servant songs of Isaiah and the redeeming passion of Christ (Acts 3:13, 26; 4:27, 30). When Matthew recorded the way in which Jesus communicated his own forgiveness and healing to the sick and suffering, he wrote: 'This was to fulfil what had been spoken through the prophet Isaiah, "He took our infirmities and bore our diseases."' (Matthew 8:17) As the first Christians moved out into evangelism, part of the saving Gospel they proclaimed of Jesus the Messiah was that he was the fulfilment of the prophetic word of the Old Testament, and of the age-old dreams of the human heart. Jesus was the Suffering Servant, the righteous One who could enter compassionately into the sorrows, pain and sins of his people, actually bearing them all away in his own living, suffering and dying.

When Philip the evangelist was led by the Spirit to the chariot of the Ethiopian eunuch, he found him meditating on a scroll of Isaiah. The eunuch was evidently a God-fearer, if not a proselyte to Judaism, but he was perplexed about the vicarious suffering described in the passage he was reading. Soon Philip was sitting with him, going through the prophecy and preaching the fulfilment of Isaiah's words in Jesus the Suffering Saviour.

Philip may well have told him that Isaiah was God's servant in the prophetic role, comforting suffering Israel ravaged by the heathen Sennacherib; also that the suffering servant was Israel itself, suffering on behalf of the nations. He may have gone on to speak of the faithful suffering remnant within Israel itself which took upon itself the pain and suffering deserved by the wider disobedient Israel. But then he

153

certainly went on to show that in Jesus, the servant-messiah had become incarnate, and that he was the representative not only of Israel, but of humankind, the One who was the ultimate and supreme fulfilment of all that the prophetic word had promised, and for whom Israel had waited through the centuries.

The Church took over the servant-messiah image to portray Jesus, not the national conquering hero of Maccabean dreams, but the One who is depicted in Isaiah's Suffering Servant song. He is a prophetic human being, anointed by the Holy Spirit, with a non-assertive and healing ministry, suffering vicariously for the sins of others, meeting unbelief, rejection, condemnation and death as a criminal. But his death is seen by God as an offering for sin, an atonement for the nations, and he accomplishes God's pleasure. He is buried honourably with the rich, resurrected in glory, and his people are justified by his sacrifice.

We don't know how much Philip communicated to the eunuch, but the vicarious dying and rising of Jesus as Saviour was part of it, for soon the eunuch was asking to be identified with Jesus by baptism in his death and resurrection: 'and both of them, Philip and the eunuch, went down into the water, and Philip baptized him . . . and the eunuch went on his way rejoicing.' (Acts 8:38-39)

PRAYER

Lord Jesus, Suffering Servant of the Lord:
What mysteries of our redemption are hidden within your
  mighty work upon the cross.

You took upon yourself our infirmities, sufferings, sorrows
and sins; you made atonement for all our transgressions,
and your sacrifice was received by the Father on our
behalf.
You were exalted to the Father's glory in the power of the
Holy Spirit, and you call us to be servants in the world,
living out your redeeming love in humble service and
sacrifice.
Grant us the vision, the anointing and the sharing of such a
task, for your glory and the world's salvation. Amen.

RESPONSE

Can you think of ways in which you have suffered or may
suffer on behalf of others, in some way bearing pain, shame
or sickness for them? Does the vicarious work of Jesus on our
behalf provide an image for you to share in his work of
redemption in our world? His redemption was unique, but he
offers you a share in its outworking.

Groups
Do organizations like Amnesty International, the International
Red Cross and the Campaign for the Abolition of the Arms
Trade take upon themselves the suffering and violence of our
world as part of their ministry? What ought the Church to be
doing in these areas, and how can the Suffering Servant role
be carried out in our society?

Lent 5: Monday

Lifted up for Sinners

NUMBERS 21:4-9; JOHN 3:14-16; 12:32-33

*M*oses made a serpent of bronze, and put it upon a pole; and whenever a serpent bit someone, that person would look at the serpent of bronze and live.

Jesus said, 'Just as Moses lifted up the serpent in the wilderness, so must the Son of Man be lifted up, that whoever believes in him may have eternal life.'

The Old Testament story of the bronze serpent is very strange — especially when you think of the Jewish aversion to images. The people of Israel, travelling with Moses from Egypt to Canaan, constantly disobeyed, grumbled, quarrelled, sinned and fell into idolatry. There came a time when their sins and grumbling overflowed, and fiery serpents attacked them, until they cried to Moses, confessing their sins. The Lord instructed Moses to set up the brass serpent on a pole so that those who gazed upon it believingly would be healed. It is interesting that the writer of the Wisdom of Solomon felt a bit uneasy about this story and makes it very clear that it was not the serpent, but the Lord who healed the people, and that it was a sign to the surrounding pagans that God was the true Deliverer (Wisdom 16:5-8).

Apart from being dramatically impressed with that story as a boy, I find it intriguing that when Jesus pondered this particular passage he found in it a powerful symbol of the 'lifting up and healing' power of the cross. For if the lost, grumbling, sinful and sick people in the wilderness could 'look and live', so this strange sign of the crucified One would impart life and healing to those who would gaze upon him by faith.

I imagine Jesus discovering this portion of scripture, hearing it in the synagogue in his youth, or perhaps in his conversation with the Jewish teachers in the temple when he was twelve. The powerful image of 'lifting up and healing' impressed itself upon him, and in his conversation with Nicodemus, who would know the story well, he used it to indicate something of the deep mystery of the passion and glory which was to come.

Then later, when his soul was deeply troubled, and he raised his heart to the Father in the hour of need, the divine voice spoke to assure and strengthen him, and he turned to the people and said, 'And I, when I am lifted up from the earth, will draw all people to myself,' and John adds: 'He said this to indicate the kind of death he was to die.' (12:32-33)

John uses an important Greek verb for the 'lifting up' of Jesus, and there is a deliberate ambiguity about it, referring both to his being lifted up on the cross and lifted up in glory. These two aspects of the 'glorifying' of Jesus in cross and exaltation are inextricably connected. The same word, meaning lifted up to glory, is found in other parts of the New

157

Testament: 'Being therefore *exalted* at the right hand of God, and having received from the Father the promise of the Holy Spirit . . .' (Acts 2:33), and 'God also highly *exalted* him and gave him the name that is above every name . . .' (Philippians 2:9).

This is not only powerful Johannine theology, but it is important for us in our experience of the darkness of our cross and passion – for there is glory on ahead for the believing soul. There is no way to glory save through the cross, and if the cross is willingly, even gladly, accepted for the sake of others, then the path of sorrow lifts you up to glory. How strange it is that the Roman gibbet, the hated instrument of execution, should become the sign and symbol of our salvation. John goes on to say: 'For God so loved the world that he gave his only Son, so that everyone who believes in him may not perish but may have eternal life.' (3:16)

PRAYER

Lord Jesus, lifted up for sinners:
You were lifted up onto the cross so that we might behold
  your suffering for our sins;
You were lifted up in exalted glory so that we might gaze
  upon your power to save and heal us.
Enable us, as we draw near to the cross, to walk humbly in
  your footsteps, to trust you unwaveringly in the days of
  darkness, and to be drawn more and more to the light
  which pierces the darkness of Calvary. Amen.

RESPONSE

Open your hymn book to the hymn 'When I survey the wondrous cross' and place beside it an empty cross or crucifix. Then reflect upon the story in today's scripture passage, and read or sing the hymn quietly. It was out of such reflection that Jesus was enabled to see that the 'lifting up' of suffering was the 'lifting up' of glory. This is what we should be affirming at this point in Lent, and in our own experience.

Lent 5: Tuesday

Into the Pit

GENESIS 37:1-28; ACTS 7:9-14

They saw [Joseph] from a distance, and conspired to kill him . . . So when Joseph came to his brothers, they stripped him of his robe, the long robe with sleeves that he wore; and they took him and threw him into a pit. . . . When some Midianite traders passed by, they drew Joseph up, lifting him out of the pit, and sold him to the Ishmaelites for twenty pieces of silver.

The Joseph cycle of stories is a narrative of great beauty and universal human application. It was part of the Jewish psyche, and a providential witness of the salvation history which Stephen could recite with pride and excitement when he was brought before the Sanhedrin.

It is not an allegory, but there are a number of parallels which put us in mind of the greater scheme of salvation acted out in the life and death of Jesus the messiah. There was the father sending his son to seek and sustain his brothers; the son's awareness of earthly and heavenly kingdom dreams; the brother's hatred and rejection of their brother; the removal of his beautiful robe and the casting him into the pit; the betrayal into foreign hands for pieces of silver. Upon the broader canvas there is the picture of the son leaving the favour of the father and the downward journey through hatred, rejection, betrayal, pit and prison. Then the ascent, from the experience of the suffering servant to the right hand of the king's favour, and restoration to the father, having on the way become the saviour, provider and sustainer of his people.

Let us today look at the first of these parallels – the rejection of the son by his brothers. The mission of the beloved son reminds us of the Incarnation. The mission concerned the love of the father for the brothers. The sending and rejection of his son was told in parable form when Jesus spoke of the mission of the prophets, and finally the beloved son, all of whom were rejected, persecuted or killed (Matthew 21:33-46). For, 'he came to . . . his own, and his own people did not accept him.' (John 1:10)

The rejection of Jesus in the gospels is the rejection of life, light and love. Just as the brothers of Joseph were drawn into further betrayal, bargaining, lying, deceit, sorrow, and ongoing double-dealing (Genesis 37:29-35), so those who choose darkness have to settle for lives which are lacking in daily providential care through good or ill, and ultimate meaning of their lives in the world.

The story of Joseph can only be understood backwards. In retrospect, all the humbling, condescension, pit-and-prison experience, and long faithfulness in trial – all this falls into place when seen from the vantage point of the end. When the hungry, suffering and needy band of brothers confess their vulnerability and fear before the unknown Joseph, he made himself known with tears of joy, and said, 'Come closer to me . . . I am your brother Joseph whom you sold into Egypt. And

161

now, do not be distressed or angry with yourselves, because you sold me here; for God sent me before you to preserve life . . . So it was not you who sent me here but God.' (45:4-8)

We should be faithful in days of light and darkness, through joys and trials, in good days and bad, for we cannot see the hidden plan of God unfolding, and often 'behind a frowning providence he hides a smiling face'. If we follow Jesus, who learned his own obedience on the path of suffering (Hebrews 5:8), we shall share with him his passion and death, and enter with him into eternal glory.

As we approach Holy Week we shall become more aware of the deepening darkness, but we shall also feel the inevitability of the divine love and passion that drove Jesus to the cross, in spite of all the shame, indignity and agony on the way. It doesn't make sense at this point on the Lenten pilgrimage, but as the glory of the end-time suddenly glances on our present path, we shall be able to go on – and trust to the end.

PRAYER

Lord Jesus, rejected by sinners:
You saw that the will of your Father was the way of the
    cross. For love of his will, and for the salvation of sinners,
    you walked the way of sorrow, pain and sacrifice.
Grant that we may no longer reject you, compromise, betray
    and sell you for material gain, but let the light of the
    ultimate glory shine upon our Lenten path, so that with
    courage and hope we may continue to the end. Amen.

162

RESPONSE

Look back upon personal experiences which at the time seemed negative periods of deprivation, suffering or perplexity. Do some of them now seem worthwhile in the light of present knowledge? Think of some of your present difficulties, misunderstandings, privations which hem you in or allow no clear direction for the future. Can you affirm the possibility of hidden providence in some of this, holding you back from wrong decisions or indicating a different direction?

Groups
Share experiences, listen to other people's experiences and let their stories light up your own.

Lent 5: Wednesday

Lamb of God

EXODUS 12:1-13; 1 CORINTHIANS 5:7-8;

REVELATION 5:6-14

*T*hen *I heard every creature in heaven and on earth and under the sea and in the sea, and all that is in them, singing: 'To the one seated on the throne and to the Lamb be blessing and honour and glory and might for ever and ever!' And the four living creatures said, 'Amen!' And the elders fell down and worshipped.*

Jesus is the Lamb of God, the counterpart and fulfilment of the Old Testament lamb, ending the regime of blood sacrifices and animal offerings. The teaching is clear and beautiful.

Jesus is the gentle lamb. He is silent, unresisting, led to slaughter (Isaiah 53:7; Jeremiah 11:19). The meekness and tenderness of Jesus is spelled out in these prophetic pictures. Katharine Tynan catches the mood in her poem 'All in the April evening':

The lambs were weary and crying
  With a weak, human cry.

164

I thought on the Lamb of God
  Going meekly to die.

Jesus is the Paschal Lamb, slain at the Passover (John 19:14-15). When the blood of the lamb was shed and painted on doorposts and lintels (Exodus 12:1-13), the Jews who sheltered under that precious blood were saved from the destroyed angel. It was John the Baptist who made the first clear identification, linking the sacrificial with the sin-bearing aspects: 'Here is the Lamb of God who takes away the sin of the world.' (John 1:29) The early Church reflects on this picture in 1 Peter 1:18-19: 'You know that you were ransomed . . . not with perishable things like silver or gold, but with the precious blood of Christ, like that of a lamb without defect or blemish.'

The multiplication of blood sacrifices in the Old Testament must have been abhorrent, with the daily repetition of the killing of many thousands of lambs through the year and especially at Passover time. Such blood sacrifices, says the writer to the Hebrews, can never take away sin (Hebrews 10:4). Christ's one sacrifice put away the old economy with one stroke.

Once, only once, and once for all,
  His precious life he gave;
Before the Cross in faith we fall,
  And own it strong to save.

Jesus is the Lamb of Adoration. Handel's 'Worthy is the Lamb' is the powerful chorus which is the climax of his *Messiah*. The words are from the Apocalypse, where Jesus is given the 'lamb' title twenty-nine times. He is the lamb upon the throne, alone worthy to receive the adoration of the whole created order, having redeemed the cosmos and become the centre of universal adoration.

These pictures of Jesus as the Lamb of God are all brought together in that wonderful eucharistic moment when the words of the *Agnus Dei* are sung gloriously in Bach's B Minor Mass, or even said quietly at a simple parish eucharist.

During my six months' solitude on the Lleyn Peninsula, I remember clearly one cold, windy, winter day, the rain lashing around the cottage. Toward evening it became dark and menacing, as it can be on that peninsula, so I placed a small light on the broad window-sill which overlooked a sloping, grassy area. When I next looked out through the wind and rain, there was a yearling lamb, soaked and huddled against the low wall. The solitude, the darkening sky, the wind, the rain, the tiny lamp – and the lamb. I was brought to tears in those moments, for the symbolism of Jesus, the Lamb of God, was there before me – its gentleness, innocence, sacrifice, obedience and patience.

I sang the *Agnus Dei*, took up my pen and wrote the poem which follows as our prayer and Response today.

LAMB ON THE ANELOG MOUNTAIN

Perched on the side of the Anelog mountain
On the tip of the Lleyn Peninsula
Facing the numinous Island of Bardsey
Called Ynys Enlli, Island of twenty thousand saints,
Stands a soft, white, silent, woolly lamb.

Winter wind howls around the tiny cottage,
Mist swirls past, enveloping Anelog in clouds,
The rain is lashed by the wind,
But the lamb stands, wind-swept, wet and alone,
Looking towards my lighted window.

He does not initiate movement
But under the poor shelter of the low stone wall
Stands unsteadily, patiently, attentively,
Against the cold, wet buffeting,
Attracted by the movement and the window lamp

Agnus Dei, qui tollis peccata mundi,
Lamb of God, by your very persistence,
By your patience, your expectation,
Your attention and concrete presence
You draw me to gaze through the window.

Miserere nobis — *have mercy upon us.*
Lamb of God, why do you stand so patiently
When I am so restless and uncertain?
Why do you gaze upon me so searchingly?
Is it reproach or silent yearning that you stand so?

Dona nobis pacem. *The elements swirl about you,*
Shrieking wind, soaking rain, and ragged mists,
Yet you stand patiently, offering me your peace,
Your silence bearing eloquent witness,
Your stillness enveloping you and me in mystery.

Dear lamb, why am I so immensely moved?
Why does my pulse quicken so?
Why do tears spring to my eyes?
Solitary lamb, straying on Anelog mountain,
In your presence I stand before the Lamb of God.

Lent 5: Thursday

Prophet of God

DEUTERONOMY 18:15; ACTS 3:17-26;

HEBREWS 1:1-2

God fulfilled what he had foretold through all the prophets, that his Messiah would suffer. Repent, therefore, and turn to God so that your sins may be wiped out, so that times of refreshing may come from the presence of the Lord, and that he may send the Messiah appointed for you, that is, Jesus, who must remain in heaven until the time of universal restoration that God announced long ago through his holy prophets. Moses said, 'The Lord your God will raise up for you from your own people a prophet like me. You must listen to whatever he tells you'.

When Peter stood up to preach at the beginning of the Church's ministry, he proclaimed Jesus as the fulfilment of God's prophetic word and as the prophet predicted by Moses (Acts 3:22-23). When Stephen stood up before the Sanhedrin he proclaimed the same thing (Acts 7:37). It was because of this prophetic tradition that the first believers felt themselves to be the inheritors: 'Long ago God spoke to our ancestors in many and various ways by the prophets, but in these last days he has spoken to us by a Son, whom he appointed heir of all things, through whom also he created the worlds.' (Hebrews 1:22)

The role of a priest is to stand before God on behalf of the people, but the role of a prophet is to stand before the people on behalf of God. The prophet was the bearer of the word of God, and in the Hebrew mind the 'word' was not simply a verbal communication which could be lost on the wind, but a creative, accomplishing word by which the world was made (Genesis 1:3), and which would bring about God's determined will (Isaiah 55:11).

It may seem strange that Christ as Prophet should be found under our week's theme, Man of Sorrows, but you only have to remember Jeremiah, the weeping prophet, and the Book of Lamentations to realize that the prophet participated in the kind of corporate personality that we moderns have lost by the way. He felt in his soul that he was one with his people, weeping, mourning, repenting for them, and smitten by the burning holiness of God against sin: 'Woe is me! I am lost, for I am a man of unclean lips, and I live among a people of unclean lips; yet my eyes have seen the King, the Lord of hosts!' (Isaiah 6:5) The bearer of the prophetic word, the revelation of God to his people, is burdened continually, not only with the weight of the divine commission, but with the sinfulness, the stubbornness and the indifference of the people.

Jesus' office as prophet also carried a divine authority lacking in the ecclesiastics of his day: 'The crowds were astounded at his teaching, for he taught them as one having authority, and not as their scribes.' (Matthew 7:28-29) Thus, his words were self-validating, and before his authoritative command sins were absolved, sickness was healed and devils fled in terror.

Jesus was aware that his ministry was a fulfilment of the whole prophetic tradition: 'Do not think that I have come to abolish the Law or the prophets; I have not come to abolish but to fulfil.' (Matthew 5:17) He did not point to the old prophets and say, 'Observe them', or 'This is my interpretation of the truth', but 'I am the Truth – follow me.'

His ministry as the revealer of God means that we discern the nature and character of God through the prophetic Christ. For example, a new ethical principle of the kingdom is enunciated when Jesus took Moses' 'eye for eye, tooth for tooth, life for life' and superseded it with love and forgiveness for enemies (Matthew 5:38-45). Or, when faced with the disciples quoting Elijah to justify calling fire down from heaven, in order to have a precedent for destroying the opposing Samaritans, Jesus answered, 'You do not know what spirit you are of, for the Son of Man has not come to destroy the lives of human beings but to save them.' (Luke 9:55)

Jesus therefore becomes, for us, the revelation of the heart of God. When Philip asked that the Father be shown to them, Jesus could have secondarily pointed him to the great prophetic tradition, but instead he affirmed the primacy of himself as the revelation of the Father: 'Whoever has seen me has seen the Father. How can you say, "Show us the Father"? Do you not believe that I am in the Father and the Father is in me?' (John 14:9-10)

The pre-incarnate Christ was present in the old prophets imparting spiritual discernment concerning himself (1 Peter 1:10-11); he was the great prophet of fulfilment during his

171

earthly ministry. He continues his prophetic ministry today (John 16:12-15), leading us, by the Holy Spirit, ever more deeply into the mystery of the love of God.

PRAYER

Lord Jesus, Prophet and revealer of God:
We look upon your face and see the glory of the Father; we
*   follow your deeds and observe the compassion of the*
*   Father; we listen to your word and are filled with the*
*   knowledge of the Father's loving heart toward sinners.*
May your word sound in us savingly, Lord Jesus; grant us
*   illuminated minds and obedient hearts, until the*
*   knowledge of the Lord covers the earth as the waters cover*
*   the sea. Amen.*

RESPONSE

Can you see the difference between the old prophetic word, which communicated God's word as far as the people of the time were able to receive it (cf. Moses), and the fulfillment of the prophetic office in Christ for us today? How do you, then, derive ethical principles from scripture?

Groups

How can the Church become the prophetic instrument of God for our day? Are there elements of judgement and mercy to be proclaimed for our generation? Is it possible for the Church to proclaim the prophetic word of Christ and for it to be rejected by society at large? Can (and ought) this to result in persecution of the Church by the world? In what circumstances?

Lent 5: Friday

Great High Priest

HEBREWS 4:14-16; 5:1-10

Since, then, we have a great high priest who has passed through the heavens, Jesus, the Son of God, let us hold fast to our confession. For we do not have a high priest who is unable to sympathize with our weaknesses, but we have one who in every respect has been tested, as we are, yet without sin. Let us therefore approach the throne of grace with boldness, so that we may receive mercy and find grace to help in time of need.

When I was Anglican chaplain at Glasgow University, I once went to a Christian Union meeting where a 'Plymouth Brother' gave a very good talk about the garments and rituals of the Old Testament priest and their symbolic meaning in Christ. He asked us to sing a hymn which only he and I, and one or two 'Brethren' Christians, knew. It became clear that only the few of us understood anything of what he said. Most of the CU members were solid Presbyterians and had never before heard such teaching. (I thought it a pity they had not discovered William Barclay's excellent *Letter to the Hebrews*.)

The Brethren speaker had immersed himself in what he

called 'The typical teaching of the Tabernacle in the Wilderness', an area which I knew well. Of course, in my Cathedral worship I was also used to eucharistic vestments, lights and incense. So we had a very good exchange of conversation on Christ the Great High Priest, and we sang with real warmth the hymn by Isaac Watts:

With joy we meditate the grace
  Of our High Priest above;
His heart is made of tenderness,
  And ever yearns with love.

Touched with a sympathy within,
  He knows our feeble frame:
He knows what sore temptations mean,
  For he has felt the same.

He in the days of feeble flesh
  Poured out his cries and tears;
And, though exalted, feels afresh
  What every member bears.

Then let our humble faith address
  His mercy and his power:
We shall obtain delivering grace
  In the distressing hour.

We learned yesterday that a prophet is one who stands before the people for God. So today we learn that a priest is one who stands before God for the people. This means that we have *access* to God through the mediatorship of Jesus our Great High Priest. The Latin word for priest is *pontifex*, literally, bridge-builder. There is a chasm of estrangement and sin between the holy God and sinful human beings. Christ, the bridge-builder, 'bridges the gulf', laying one hand upon the holy throne of God and the other upon his erring brothers and sisters. And because our priest is human, he feels our weaknesses, sympathizes with our helplessness, and bears our infirmities.

One of the lovely pictures of the Old Testament High Priest is when he stands before God as the representative of Israel, clothed in his garments of glory and beauty. On his shoulders he wears two onyx stones, each inscribed with six of the tribes of Israel, and on his breastplate are set twelve precious stones, each inscribed with the name of one of the twelve tribes. So too Christ, our High Priest, bears us on his shoulders, the place of strength, and upon his heart, the place of love, as he intercedes for us before the great Father of mercy.

All God's people are believer-priests by virtue of their baptism, but those who are called to the ministry of priesthood within the Church of God undergo training. I do not speak here of theological seminary and intellectual study (which are, of course, necessary), but of the profound training by the Holy Spirit. This involves the painful joy of bearing another's burdens, standing in the holy presence, pleading with groaning and tears for the world's sin. A lack of this kind of training produces superficial priests who do not know what they are about. The pattern is the school of Jesus:

In the days of his flesh, Jesus offered up prayers and supplications with loud cries and tears, to the one who was able to save him from death, and he was heard because of his reverent submission. Although he was a Son, he learned obedience through what he suffered; and having been made perfect, he became the source of eternal salvation for all who obey him, having been designated by God a high priest according to the order of Melchizedek.

This reference to Melchizedek was to show that Christ's priesthood was not according to the mortal Order of Aaron, for that priesthood was finite, needing to offer continual sacrifices and even sin offerings for its own faults. Christ's is an eternal and unchanging priesthood, based on the one, complete and single offering for ever – a priesthood which he shares with his people. This priestly ministry of Christ did not end with his sacrificial offering of his life in death and resurrection, but continues now as he stands before the Father as our faithful High Priest, drawing us into the life of intercession and adoration with him.

Not only do the intercessions of Christ as our Advocate (1 John 2:1) guarantee our forgiveness and the blessings of the Holy Spirit, but we have boldness before God, to enter in meditative and contemplative prayer, for we are caught up in the mighty river of communion and adoration which flows between the Father and the Son in the power of the Holy Spirit. Even our weak prayers are energized by the Spirit, and the ignorance of our prayers are interpreted and offered by the Saviour.

All God's people, then, share in the priesthood of Christ. Therefore we have our place before God to intercede for our lost world. We are called to bear the sorrows, infirmities, sufferings and sins of our world, to offer them to God through our Great High Priest, releasing salvation, healing and access to the glory of the Father for all who will come.

PRAYER

Jesus, our Great High Priest:
You bear us before God as our Priest and Mediator; you lay
down your life as sacrifice and victim;
In you, Lord Jesus, we have access, by the Holy Spirit, to the
Father, and receive the grace of absolution, a new heart of
love, and a part in your priestly work in the world.
Bestow on us the peace which comes after absolution, the
assurance of your forgiving presence, and a deeper
understanding of the priestly vocation to which you have
called us on behalf of our sinful and suffering world. Amen.

RESPONSE

If all Christ's baptized disciples share his priesthood, how can the particular calling to be ordained priest in the Church of God truly function within this Church of believer-priests?

Groups

How do you see your personal and group priesthood functioning in your street, neighbourhood or parish? In which ways can you bear the sorrow, tears and hardships of others in your heart, showing sympathy towards them and intercession for them? Can you answer these questions on a devotional and a practical level?

Lent 5: Saturday

The Second Adam

ROMANS 5:12-21; 1 CORINTHIANS 15:21-22, 45-49

*A*s all die in Adam, so all will be made alive in Christ
. . . Thus it is written: 'The first man Adam became a
living being'; the last Adam became a life-giving spirit.
. . . The first man was from the earth, a man of dust; the
second man is from heaven. . . . Just as we have borne the
image of the man of dust, we will also bear the image of the
man of heaven.

While I was struggling with my thesis on 'The Concept of
God in the Theology of John A. T. Robinson' in Zurich in
what seems a lifetime ago, my Norwegian fellow student
Peder was grappling with the difficult Greek text and exegesis
of 'The Adam-Christ Parallel' of today's passages. You can
witness how difficult Paul's thinking is even in the English of
Romans 5:12-21, with sentences left in the air and a context
which was familiar to the Jewish mind, but not easy for us.
Nevertheless, these passages are theologically vital, and
devotionally rewarding.

Jesus as the Second Adam illustrates our week's theme
because it deals with the human dilemma, our fallen

condition, and its redemption. If the difficult theological arguments contained in the above passages are reduced to one sentence it is found in Paul's words: 'As all die in Adam, so all will be made alive in Christ.'

The kind of Jewish contextual thinking that Paul was addressing was one in which Adam's pride, rebellion and sinful tendency has been communicated to the whole of humanity. Take these words from the period between the Old and New Testaments:

> The first Adam, burdened with an evil heart, transgressed and was overcome, as were also all who were descended from him. . . . A grain of evil seed was sown in Adam's heart from the beginning, and how much ungodliness it has produced until now – and will produce until the time of threshing comes! (2 Esdras 3:21; 4:30)

The basic concept in Paul's mind is the solidarity of the human race – we are all one. We are 'one with' Adam and 'one with' Christ in our common humanity.

This way of thinking is not immediately familiar to us because we have lost our way in our egocentric individualism. We are afflicted by a modern, western disease by which we have become fragmented, divided and alienated. We can no longer feel our primitive tribal solidarity of belonging to the clan or family, much less the human race. We have become separated islands in an ocean of restlessness and loneliness. Perhaps the best exponents of this alienated human dilemma are the existentialist novelists like Jean Paul Sartre and Andre Gide, who may not be able to give us a healing prescription,

181

but diagnose the human condition with painful, realistic situations from which there is no exit.

I must say, on a personal level, that I have been profoundly helped by Fr Christopher Bryant's exposition of Carl Jung's concept of the personal and collective unconscious mind in the area of Christian spirituality. It was Fr Bryant who first encouraged me to write, and I remember the excitement I felt in first reading his *Depth Psychology and Religious Belief*. This is a good way in which to help us understand the solidarity implicit in our humanity, before we go on to try and grasp corporate personality in the Old Testament prophets.

If we are 'in Adam' we are involved with all that marks the fallenness of our humanity. The Bible teaches an 'original innocence' as the primary reality, but sin, brokenness and enmity soon come on the scene, leaving a trail of disintegration down the ages. The human family is separated from God; relationships within the family are ruptured by pride, jealousy, greed and all the elements of our disordered humanity. Every human being, within himself or herself, experiences a loss of unified vitality and integrity, and is subject to finitude and mortality.

But if we are 'in Christ' we come to understand and experience that he is the 'Second Adam', the federal Head of our humanity. From him flows the redemption and restoration that heals the broken image of God within us. We are 'ransomed, healed, restored, forgiven', and our relationship with God is made new through our Saviour and Mediator, Jesus. If Jesus is the Man of Sorrows he is also the Man of Glory, communicating to those who are united in solidarity with him all the blessings of the new creation – the healing of the mortal wound of sin by his atoning death and resurrection.

Paul's conclusion is that if we have borne the sorrowful image of the earthly Adam, we may also bear the glorious image of the heavenly Adam. So our Lenten journey becomes one from earth to glory, by the grace of the New Adam who is Christ.

PRAYER

Lord Jesus, heavenly Adam:
We are conscious of the brokenness and alienation of our
human nature when we fall into sin, failure and broken
relationships; we are also bowed down by our mortality in
sickness and the fear of death.
Enable us, dear Lord, to find in you our heavenly Adam, the
physician who heals our wounds, the Saviour who forgives
our sins, the Mediator who restores our relationship with
God, and so renews the brokenness of our humanity until we
are all reconciled in your eternal kingdom of Love. Amen.

RESPONSE

If we are one race, in solidarity with every other man, woman and child in our world, then it should be possible for each of us to relate to one another on the common ground of our one humanity. Such an understanding of solidarity means that we can increase the amount of good in our world as we share hope, sympathy and understanding, so that the love of God may reach our brothers and sisters everywhere.

Groups

Listen and share your thoughts with each other about the reality of 'belonging' to one global family. What does this say about race-relations, gender, nationalism, about economic equality and sharing? And how does the group actually carry out these principles in action?

HOLY WEEK

Jesus, Man of Majesty

He set his face towards Jerusalem.

Holy Week: Palm Sunday

The Way of Love

ZECHARIAH 9:9-10; LUKE 19:28-41

As Jesus rode along, people kept spreading their cloaks on the road. As he was now approaching the path down from the Mount of Olives, the whole multitude of the disciples began to praise God joyfully with a loud voice for all the deeds of power that they had seen . . . Some of the Pharisees in the crowd said to him, 'Teacher, order your disciples to stop.' He answered, 'I tell you if these were silent, the stones would cry out.'

We have noted that there is a strong prophetic objection to empty liturgy and ritual that lacks integrity and merely sustains pious hypocrisy (Isaiah 1:12-17). But there is liturgical integrity when worship and celebration combine in an act of sheer joy, or even in genuine sorrow, and the outcome is a life closer to God in the sharing of his joy and sorrow. This week is filled with this kind of liturgical participation in many churches. In parishes, convents and monasteries I have shared in the Palm Sunday liturgy, which I find increasingly meaningful. It moves from processional joy at the outset, through the dramatic reading or singing of the Passion gospel to an awareness that the shadow of the cross is beginning to dominate Holy Week. This day is the anticipation of it all: the Palm Sunday Procession.

I remember one beautiful Palm Sunday morning at St Margaret's, Upper Norwood, when we set out with the processional cross, palm leaves and catkin branches, in a joyful congregation of men, women and children. It was a lively and happy procession, singing 'All glory, laud and honour' around the recreation field and back to the church for the eucharist. The people of the neighbourhood who had not come to church that morning looked from their doors and windows at this remarkable procession of joyful celebration. We didn't have a donkey with us that year, but it got us in the mood to understand what was happening from Bethany to Jerusalem on that first Palm Sunday.

First of all, Jesus was fulfilling prophecy. Zechariah's words were in the minds of the people who welcomed him, laying their garments and branches in the way as they greeted him in the messianic words of Psalm 118. Secondly, if Jesus was entering the holy city as Messiah, he was spelling out the *kind* of messiah – not a conquering hero riding upon a war horse, but the Prince of Peace riding upon a donkey. Of course, many in the crowd were simply sightseers who could be swayed one way or the other; and some cherished the patriotic, even zealot, dreams of a warrior-messiah. But Jesus made his claim clear to the wider group of disciples who cried out with joy and hope as he rode purposely, courageously, into the city which promised him betrayal and death.

It is at this point that the mood changes dramatically. The representatives of authority are there, and they hate the joyful celebration. They are madly jealous of this kindly man of peace, and call on Jesus to stop the singing and stifle the excitement. Jesus looks at them with deep sorrow and says, 'I tell you, if these were silent, the stones would cry out.' The next sentence goes on: 'As he came near and saw the city, he wept over it.' This is where we begin the drama of Holy Week, and the dual mingling of sadness and glory is expressed in the hymn for Psalm Sunday:

> Ride on! ride on in majesty!
>   In lowly pomp ride on to die:
> O Christ, your triumph now begin
>   O'er captive death and conquered sin.

PRAYER

> Lord Jesus, King and Messiah:
> You rode the way of sorrow before you entered into glory;
>   you tasted the pain of suffering before you shared the
>   wine of gladness.
> Enable us to accompany you this week on the Way of
>   Sorrows to the cross, that we may at last enter into the
>   city of Peace. Amen.

RESPONSE

If your parish celebrates this day with a Palm Procession and eucharist, prepare yourself by reading, prayerfully, the parallel accounts in the four gospels of Jesus' entry into Jerusalem.

Groups

Let the group members prepare for the meeting by imagining themselves in the different parts of the story privately, then sharing in the group how they felt. Let the meeting end with a reading of G. K. Chesterton's poem 'The Donkey'.

Holy Week: Monday

The Way of Peter

MATTHEW 26:31-35, 69-75

*P*eter said to him, 'Though all become deserters because of you, I will never desert you.'

Jesus said to him, 'Truly I tell you, this very night, before the cock crows, you will deny me three times.'

Peter said to him, 'Even though I must die with you, I will not deny you.'

. . . Then Peter began to curse, and he swore an oath, 'I do not know the man!' At that moment the cock crowed. Then Peter remembered what Jesus had said: 'Before the cock crows, you will deny me three times.' And he went out and wept bitterly.

Peter was utterly sincere, not lacking in moral courage, and loving Jesus so much that he wanted to take that ultimate step, make that supreme sacrifice. Oh yes! There were moments of rash boldness, of sanguine determination, of emotional commitment. Not even the knowing, cautioning, restraining words of Jesus could dampen his enthusiasm or cause him to take a long, hard look at his motivation, his measure of resolve. For this was a time for affirmation, in order to lift the burdened spirit of Jesus – and he was the man to do it.

It all came to nothing. No, worse than that. It came to a shadowy and shabby denial before the bystanders and the serving girls. As he was pressed, the denial became an oath, and the oath turned to cursing and swearing, until he was pulled up short by the sound of the cock crowing. Then came the desolation, the burdened grief and the scalding tears. Luke captures a heart-rending moment for both of them as Jesus is led out of the high priest's house: 'The Lord turned and looked at Peter. Then Peter remembered . . . and went out and wept bitterly.' (22:61-62)

Why is it that these two moments in Peter's experience are so powerful in the portrayal of a man who loved, and a man who denied his love? I believe that it is because the accounts must have come from Peter himself. There is a simple integrity which lends pathos and power to the accounts. It is living experience which is communicated through sorrow and tears.

Then there is the reader's immediate response to these two situations. These stories grab me because they draw me into the narrative. I become present because I am Peter. At the beginning of Holy Week I make my emotional affirmations. I assure the Messiah in the wake of Palm Sunday that I am with him, I will stand by him, and if necessary, I will die for him. This is a genuine mirror image of my feelings and experience – *sometimes*.

But there are other times. That time of waiting in the twilight of the courtyard, while the flames of the open fire are dancing in the shadows; that sudden, unprepared, unexpected moment when Peter is confronted by a simple servant girl, and his relationship with the prisoner who at this moment is being tried in the priest's house is challenged. His denial simply tumbles out; he is covered with confusion, embarrassment, perplexity. The accusation is taken up by the bystanders, and Peter feels the cold sweat in his armpits and down his back as avowals of ignorance and denial turn to oaths and curses. I've been there too, and my denials have been by words, acts and silences.

There it is. The devastating honesty and integrity of the account, washed in penitence and tears, and set down with no self-justification or excuses. That's where we are in Holy Week.

But that is not the end of the story. There is another narrative of affirmation, but this time it is Peter's humbled and penitent response to forgiveness and love (John 21:15-17). But we cannot take that jump today.

Today we are on the last lap of that journey which leads us up to the hill called Calvary. Today we enter more deeply into the meaning of the cross, and realize a little more clearly our own denials of love – and yet Jesus looks upon us in compassion and understanding. We stand with Peter at the beginning of Holy Week and sing quietly the words which another great sinner wrote out of his own experience:

> *Amazing grace! how sweet the sound*
> *That saved a wretch like me;*
> *I once was lost, but now am found;*
> *Was blind, but now I see.*

PRAYER

Lord Jesus, victim and prisoner:

*You were persecuted, ill-treated, by the powers and ruling
authorities of your day, and still you suffer the same
victimization and torture in all the injustices of our
world.*

*When Peter denied you by word and deed, great sorrow and
grief filled his soul, and you led him through penitence
and tears, back to your loving heart.*

*Let us not stand by, allowing you to suffer in the innocent
victims of our day, by our words, deeds and silences.
Strengthen us by your Spirit to make our affirmations
with courage and understanding, free from the moral
cowardice that comes so easily to us.* Amen.

RESPONSE

Recall experiences where you have affirmed your loyalty and
then fallen into denial, neglect or even cowardly desertion of
people and promises. As Peter sought honestly and humbly to
take the path of penitence and restitution, can you see your
way to redeem past sins and mistakes by the strength of
Christ?

Groups

Consider situations in which the Church or society has denied
basic human rights and compassion to poor and deprived

minorities. Are you informed/involved with agencies which bring relief and restitution? Penitence must result in putting right past failures, but without bitterness and by the grace of Christ.

Holy Week: Tuesday

The Way of Judas

MATTHEW 26:14-25, 47-56; 27:3-10

Judas, one of the Twelve, arrived; with him was a large crowd with swords and clubs, from the chief priests and the elders of the people. Now the betrayer had given them a sign, saying, 'The one I will kiss is the man; arrest him.' At once he came up to Jesus and said, 'Greetings, Rabbi!' and kissed him. Jesus said to him, 'Friend, do what you are here to do.' Then they came and laid hands on Jesus and arrested him.

When Judas, his betrayer, saw that Jesus was condemned, he repented and brought back the thirty pieces of silver to the chief priests and the elders. He said, 'I have sinned by betraying innocent blood.' But they said, 'What is that to us? See to it yourself.' Throwing down the pieces of silver in the temple, he departed, and he went and hanged himself.

Last evening, as I finished writing about the denial and restoration hope of Peter, the ending of the day was soft with early spring sunshine, giving way to an almost mystical colouring of the fields around and sky above. This morning the sun was seen to rise, but over the last half hour it has become dark and cold with a rising wind and rain. This is a Judas day.

Faced with the person of Judas I am perplexed, distressed and deeply troubled, for he mirrors to me what our humanity is capable of in its darkest moments. This is a world in which we are capable of a Jewish Holocaust in Germany, of the systematic killing of millions of Soviet citizens under Stalin, of nuclear warfare in Hiroshima and Nagasaki, of the plunder of what we call the third world, reducing and keeping it in poverty while we line our own 'developed' pockets.

Faced with Judas' treachery in betraying the Lord and Saviour who loved him, the question 'why?' stands out in bold relief. The answers reflect more the mind and temperament of the questioners than an objective pursuit of truth which leads to unknowing.

This is especially true when we come across a devotional meditation which portrays Judas as so filled with self-loathing and remorse that he rushes to hang himself before Jesus actually dies, so that he may run to the Saviour in the intermediate state after death and fall before him, pleading forgiveness and restoration. Let us look at what some people have said.

First, Judas was a Judean among Galilean disciples, and he may well have been the most discerning among them. Perhaps he mixed nationalistic sympathies with ambition, and as he saw increasingly what kind of messiah Jesus was, he may have been bitterly disappointed. Jesus transformed the popular meaning of messiah from a nationalistic, conquering hero to a suffering servant-king whose kingdom was not territory, power and political influence, but justice, mingled with mercy and gentleness. This was not Judas' way, and he sold such a messiah to death.

Or Judas may have seen Jesus as a reluctant messiah,

needing to be pushed, forced, catapulted into a crisis which would compel him to show his hand. So he organized the arrest in Gethsemane in order that Jesus would use his messianic and charismatic powers to call into action the zealots who were waiting for such a man and such a moment.

Others have thought of Judas engineering the arrest by the authorities in order to protect Jesus from an assassin's hand, or to prevent Jesus and the disciples from provoking a stupid and futile bloody insurrection which would come to nothing. Some have even thought that Judas suddenly realized the shadow of death was upon them all because of Jesus' actions, and simply funked it, betraying Jesus in cowardice to save his own skin.

Traditionally Judas has been thought of as a scheming, ambitious thief, tempted by power and money, secretly thieving from the common purse and yielding at last to a financial transaction. He was led on by that dimension of spiritual darkness of which both Luke (22:3) and John (13:27) report: that 'Satan entered in Judas'. The gospel writers proclaim the good news that the human heart may welcome the Holy Spirit of God and be indwelt by the compassion and charism of Jesus the Saviour. But there is also this dark dimension of demonic influence and possession which is at work at the very heart of the apostolic band, corrupting the core of vowed discipleship, fulfilling the prophetic word: 'Even my bosom friend in whom I trusted, who ate of my bread, has lifted the heel against me.' (Psalm 41:9)

Jesus never spoke more fearful words than these: 'The Son of Man goes as it is written of him, but woe to that one by whom the Son of Man is betrayed! It would have been better for that one not to have been born.' (Matthew 26:24) It is not appropriate to read into these words some double decree of predestination that damns poor Judas from all eternity, but they do ring with the warning of dark powers which attack the most pure and lovely works of God in order to corrupt, contaminate and destroy the communion of love by treachery and betrayal.

Judas became the traitor of traitors, for only a beloved friend can become a traitor. What could this have meant for Jesus who dipped his hand in the dish with Judas as a token of friendship? Had he watched the gradual, corrosive deterioration of soul that lured Judas from his first fiery enthusiasm and love for Jesus, into self-deception and demonic temptation, ambition, compromise and treachery? A double life leads to daily compromise, and surely Judas' discernment enabled him to realize that Jesus knew, and that Jesus was aware of Judas' own self-knowledge. Or was Judas lacking in self-perception because of the corruptive influence of Satan? We don't know. But how could Judas have borne the Saviour kneeling to wash his feet? How could he have reclined at table with him over the bread and wine that Jesus shared as his very body and blood? The blackest picture we have is of Judas, after receiving and swallowing the portion that Jesus gave him, immediately going out, 'and it was night' (John 13:30).

To what conclusion can we come about Judas? Matthew says that he repented, threw down the silver pieces and confessed that he had sinned in betraying innocent blood. Also, his remorse and grief led him to suicide. The religious authorities spurned such a change of mind and heart. Perhaps at the end we can only leave Judas in the hands of the all-knowing and merciful God, whose secret counsels are beyond anything that we can imagine, and to the One who prayed for his enemies as he was nailed to the cross: 'Father, forgive them; for they do not know what they are doing.' (Luke 23:34)

PRAYER

Lord Jesus, wounded in the house of your friends:
As we look into our hearts we are aware of our denials of
*   your grace, and our betrayals of your love;*
We are aware that from the very gate of heaven there is a
*   door to hell, and that in our pride and self-esteem we*
*   may be lured to treachery and corruption.*
Come, Lord Jesus, and dwell in those depths of which we are
*   hardly aware, redeem those areas of our lives which, left*
*   to us, would lead us into sin;*
Deliver us from sitting in judgement on others, and enlarge
*   our understanding of the measure of your redemption.*
*   Amen.*

RESPONSE

Reflect upon the ways in which desire for power, the lure of ambition and the greed for money has led people and nations into the compromise of loving relationships and the abuse of sacred trust.

Think of relationships which have deteriorated in your own

life, for whatever reason. A breakdown in personal relationships, or schism in the Body of Christ betrays the reconciling Saviour, and he is always ready to enable you to take the first step, pray the first prayer, offer a reconciling hand. If it is possible, take a first step today to heal the wound, to repair the brokenness.

Holy Week:
Wednesday

The Way of John

JOHN 13:21-30; 18:15-16; 21:20-25

Jesus was troubled in spirit, and declared, 'Very truly, I tell you, one of you will betray me.'

The disciples looked at one another, uncertain of whom he was speaking. One of his disciples — the one whom Jesus loved — was reclining next to him. Simon Peter therefore motioned to him to ask Jesus of whom he was speaking. So while reclining next to Jesus, he asked him, 'Lord, who is it?'

Jesus answered, 'It is the one to whom I give this piece of bread when I have dipped it in the dish.'

Simon Peter and another disciple followed Jesus. Since that disciple was known to the high priest, he went with Jesus into the courtyard . . . but Peter was standing outside at the gate. So the other disciple . . . went out and spoke to the woman who guarded the gate, and brought Peter in.

I have always been intrigued by the anonymity of this 'other disciple', the 'one whom Jesus loved', who 'reclined at his breast'. Holy Week is not the time to enter into biblical critical attitudes, right though they may be in their place, but there is

201

a strong tradition which maintains that this is John himself, and so we shall accept it for the present. In the two passages quoted above, and in the third from John, we have the same person:

> Peter turned and saw the disciple whom Jesus loved following them; he was the one who had reclined next to Jesus at the supper and had said, 'Lord who is it that is going to betray you?' When Peter saw him, he said to Jesus, 'Lord, what about him?'
>
> Jesus said to him, 'If it is my will that he should remain until I come, what is that to you? Follow me!'

There are three things I want to draw attention to about John, which causes me to pattern my discipleship of Christ upon this man.

He was the disciple that Jesus loved. This, above all, is what I found at twelve years of age. Jesus became to me Saviour, Friend and Brother, and all through my life it has been like that, and increasingly so. John's reclining upon the breast of Jesus was the mark of intimacy, communion, and mutual sharing of love and pain. Charles Mudie's words illustrate this:

> *I lift my heart to Thee,*
> *Saviour divine;*
> *For Thou art all to me,*
> *And I am Thine,*
> *Is there on earth a closer bond than this:*
> *That my Beloved's mine, and I am His?*

This illustrates the particular Johannine understanding of union with Christ, or 'mystical indwelling'. Far from being the inmost secret of the privileged elect, it is the open secret of the Gospel. The New Testament envisages every believer dwelling in Christ, and Christ dwelling in them in a real, albeit mystical, manner. It is a personal relationship of loving intimacy between Christ and the believer, and it is also the mystical communion between Christ and his Church, portrayed in the organic life of the vine and the branches (John 15:1-11).

The Johannine intimacy with Christ is offered to all who will receive it, the inflaming of two hearts in one love. I had to move on in my boyhood experience, of course, and enter into a more trinitarian understanding of the divine indwelling, and also see the corporate nature of the channelling of the mystical life of the Holy Spirit in nature, in the word, and in the sacraments. But it began there as a boy, and it continues as a basic and simple relationship of loving communion in my hermit exploration. That aspect of it is also found in the Franciscan mystic, Ramon Lull: 'The Lover longed for solitude, and went away to live alone, that he might have the companionship of his Beloved, for amid many people he was lonely.'

John followed 'closely' in his pilgrimage of discipleship. He did not allow his personal relationship with Jesus to become individualistic. He followed Christ in a faithful pilgrimage of loyalty even when and where he did not understand. Not only did he dwell close to the heart of Christ at the Last Supper, but he followed closely into the courtyard of the high priest; he followed the Way of Sorrows to Calvary, allowing Mary to lean

hard upon him, standing with her to the bitter end at the foot
of the cross. It was he who ran like the wind when he heard
Mary Magdalene's story of Jesus' rising (John 20:1-5), and it
was he who would remain to bear witness to the whole
glorious story and experience (John 21:23-25).

It is my desire to follow, not only in an inward and mystical
experience of divine and mutual indwelling, which has been my
chief joy since childhood, but also to allow my life, together
with my sisters' and brothers', to be Jesus' hands and feet in
our world. Identification with Jesus in the ordinariness, the joy,
the sorrow of the world, must be interpreted differently in
every generation. Whatever is true on a personal level, there
must be a corporate sense of Christ living within his Church
and in the human family in a reconciling and compassionate
dimension of practical service.

He was associated with Peter. Peter was meant to be the centre
of unity for the apostolic band, but John was linked to Peter
in a more human and basic manner. John slept in Gethsemane
sharing the sorrow and heaviness of Peter, and he acted on
Peter's indication in the first of today's readings. According to
John 13:25-26, he alone heard Jesus say that Judas was the
betrayer. He kept the sorrow, sharing the profound grief and
distress of Jesus, not passing it on to Peter. He also led Peter
through the gate to the high priest's courtyard when Jesus was
being tried.

Does it seem a strange thing that he actually let Peter
through the gate of temptation in the courtyard of the high
priest? It is no accident that Jesus was led to his temptation
by the Holy Spirit (Matthew 4:1). So it is a fact that we are

to be to our brothers and sisters what God would have us be: always loving, sustaining, communing, but sometimes challenging, encouraging and provoking to deeper love and dedication.

In today's final scripture passage, Peter is told by Jesus that John would 'remain' in steadfastness and loyalty. Peter is intrigued and curious about 'this man', for he must have watched closely John's profound inward transformation from son of thunder (Mark 3:17) to the beloved disciple.

So what has all this to do with me today? Well I want to discover the threefold pattern referred to in my own life. First, I am called into a profoundly personal and reciprocal love of Christ. This is not a sentimental or romantic matter, it is rather an invitation to sorrow and a challenge to courage, but also a mystical awareness of Christ living within me. Second, it involves a close following of Christ – not only to places of light, enthusiasm and joy but also into the Gethsemane places of grief and pain. And third, John's association with Peter is a symbol of my association and relationship with my brothers and sisters on the road to Calvary. It is a sharing with them in the daily struggle and hope that reaches out to one another in darkness, and moves forward the light, and ultimate glory.

PRAYER

Lord Jesus, Beloved of the Father:
There have been times when I have envied John reclining on
*   your loving heart, feeling the heartbeat of the Redeemer;*

But I have learned that it is my place too, and that it is
there that I learn to grow in the intimate loving
communion which alone can sustain my love for you in the
world.

Grant me such a sense of that divine indwelling that I may
become a true channel of your compassion, an instrument of
your grace, and a light in the world's darkness. Amen.

RESPONSE

It is clear that when Jesus most needed the comfort of loving
communion to undergird those urgent hours leading up to
Gethsemane and Calvary, there was instead perplexity, distress,
denial, betrayal and treachery. In the beloved disciple we find
one who sought simply to give himself to Christ at every level
of his life – body, soul and spirit. Will you seek to accompany
Jesus closely during these last days of Holy Week? Try to
identify areas in which God is speaking to you in a new way
at this point in your pilgrimage.

Groups
Can you see the Church's distress, uncertainty and division in
the disintegration of the disciples as they moved into
Gethsemane? Only by following the pattern of the next few
days of cross and resurrection can the Church become whole.
Ask how your group, your church fellowship, can follow that
pattern. Perhaps you could begin with the washing of feet?

Maundy Thursday

Washing of Feet

JOHN 13:1-17

Now before the festival of the Passover, Jesus knew that his hour had come to depart from this world and go to the Father. Having loved his own who were in the world, he loved them to the end. . . . And during supper, Jesus, knowing that the Father had given all things into his hands, and that he had come from God and was going to God, got up from the table, took off his outer robe, and tied a towel around himself. Then he poured water into the basin and began to wash the disciples' feet and to wipe them with the towel that was tied around him.

Maundy Thursday is the beginning of three amazing days. And in this wonderful passage of scripture the sheer wonder and beauty of the first verses are marred by the profound sadness and fearful tragedy of the malice which smouldered in Judas' heart.

Yet he was not the only cause for sadness. On the way, the disciples had been arguing over prestige, status, precedent (Luke 22:24-29). They were concerned with rank and status while the eternal issues of redeeming love and the bearing of the world's pain were pressing upon the Saviour's heart. So when they got to the upper room, this competitive atmosphere did not allow anyone to serve the others in the menial task of the washing of feet.

Jesus decided to speak such words of yearning, intimacy and loving concern to them that something immediate and radical had to be done to bring home the issues of life and death that were in the air that night. So during supper he got up, removed his robe, tied a towel around his waist and knelt before them to wash their feet. There was consternation mingled with shame, and an embarrassed silence. They were well aware of the compassionate rebuke which was double-edged in its application, and each one felt it specifically towards himself.

These last few days we have been thinking of John, of Judas and of Peter, and we can, perhaps, put ourselves in their places as Jesus moves quietly around in the pregnant atmosphere in which competitive rivalry was melting before the regal humility of our Lord's gentleness. At least Jesus was aware of the profound emotions that stirred dear John's heart to tenderness and tears, though no word is recorded.

When Jesus reached Judas he showed no anger, for he loved Judas, and he allowed his wounded heart to be exposed as he took Judas' feet in his hands, washing and drying them tenderly. And for a moment there was no one else in the room save the two of them. But the moment passed and Judas hardened his heart.

Then Jesus moved on in the silence until he came to Peter. Peter had watched with increasing discomfort and uneasiness. Then suddenly he felt Jesus' hands on his feet, and emotional and impulsive as ever he cried out, 'Lord, are you going to wash my feet?' Jesus answered, 'You do not know now what I am doing, but later you will understand.'

Perhaps we should stop here. This may be God's word for me, for you, today. There have been times when I have been perplexed, embarrassed, ashamed by the love of the Lord, and I have known the emotional turmoil both of joy and sorrow in his dealings with me. But there have also been times when I have been bewildered by the sheer contrariness of a situation which could yield no meaning in my life. And at other times there has been the independent fear of letting myself go completely into the unknown path which only Christ can control and regulate. The words are appropriate to me today in my hermitage, even as I look back over the last few years of exploration in the hermit life: 'You do not know what I am doing, but later you will understand.'

How about you? Have there been times of elation, disappointment, sickness, trial, persecution, misunderstanding, perplexity; when you have cried out in joy, in anger, in yearning, or even in ignorance? And what about today? It is the Thursday of Holy Week, and our Lord Jesus comes to you, girded with humility and tenderness, and takes your soiled feet into his hands, washing, drying, kissing and anointing them for service, for pilgrimage, for following. Will you let him do it? Will you yield, surrender, abandon pride and self-will? A certain passivity and letting-go is asked of you. There is no coercion, simply the condescension of the kneeling Lord – and the outcome depends on you.

The whole atmosphere of the upper room was transformed. Jesus resumed his place at the table again so that he could carry his disciples in word and action into the darkness and glory that lay immediately ahead. And so it is with me, and with you, today.

PRAYER

Lord Jesus, girded with humility:

It is I who should be at your feet, in penitence and adoration; but you lay aside your glory, stoop to my need and minister to my vulnerability.

As you have tenderly taken the place of lowly service to your sisters and brothers, so let me do the same;

As you transform disputes of priority and status into mutual sharing of fellowship and concern, so let me become a channel of your peace, and an instrument of your reconciliation.

For I would lay the world tenderly at your feet, as you humbled yourself at the feet of your disciples. Amen.

RESPONSE

If your church includes the simple enactment of the washing of feet in its eucharist of the Last Supper this evening, be there, and ponder on ways in which its significance indicates to you a particular act of service to your fellows.

Groups

Share in today's liturgy, and if it does not include the washing of feet, why not prepare in advance and enact the ceremony in your group? Either choose a sister or brother to carry out the foot-washing, or let there be an orderly mutual foot-washing in a circle of movement during the reading of this gospel. End with singing leading to silent reflection.

Good Friday

The Foot of the Cross

JOHN 19:16-27

When Jesus saw his mother and the disciple whom he loved standing beside her, he said to his mother, 'Woman, here is your son.' Then he said to the disciple, 'Here is your mother.' And from that hour the disciple took her into his own home.

Good Friday – a bad day if ever there was one. This was the day on which the incarnation of the divine Love was taken, unjustly condemned, beaten and cruelly crucified by the hands of his creatures. And yet it was a day so good that it manifested the length and the depth to which Love would go to reconcile the world to himself.

I had set aside this day to consider, pray and write about the dying Jesus. However, during the early hours of this morning Brother David, our ninety-four-year-old friar, died peacefully. So my thoughts and prayers are with him today at this monastery which is dedicated to St Mary at the Cross. I commend David to the loving care of his dear Saviour, and reflect upon the words in which Jesus commended his mother, Mary, to the beloved disciple, John, and John to her.

These words of commendation are engraved below the clock tower, to be seen by anyone coming up the track towards Glasshampton. It is right that brothers and retreatants coming here should have this image of 'St Mary at the Cross' before them, for the foot of the cross is not only the place of forgiveness and salvation, but the place of waiting, reflection and contemplation. As I take my place at the foot of the cross, I realize that I am not alone, for I am aware of the presence of Mary.

It had come to this at last, and in the depths of her grief and pain Mary pondered on those precious moments which had brought her to this hour. After that amazing visit by the angel Gabriel, she had conceived in her body the incarnate Son of God, and in her mind the task which had been laid upon her (Luke 1:38). Later, as she held the child in her arms she heard the wonderful story told by the shepherds of the angelic chorus, and 'she treasured all these words and pondered them in her heart.' (Luke 2:19) Then in the temple there was the early and intuitive apprehension of the pain to come when Simeon gave the baby back to her, speaking strange words of revelation: '. . . the inner thoughts of many will be revealed – and a sword will pierce your own soul too.' (Luke 2:35) All too soon, at twelve years of age among the teachers in the temple, Jesus had affirmed his own awareness of the Father's call, and at his words, 'his mother treasured all these things in her heart.' (Luke 2:51)

So it had been throughout his life, and by the time he was ready for the Jordan baptism that initiated his public ministry she felt a surge of mingled joy and sorrow. Joy, because his was the messianic vocation of deliverance for those who dwelt in

213

darkness and the shadow of death; but sorrow, because he was the suffering servant who would himself tread that dark valley, bearing the sins and sorrows of his people. And as a mother – especially *his* mother – she would share the pain. So here it was.

In no sense should we minimize the pain and reality of that heavy grief which tore her heart and numbed her mind. But the strange feeling endured that somehow this was not the end. How impossible and senseless was such a feeling in the face of the suffering and death before her very eyes – yet it persisted. In that moment she looked into the eyes of Jesus, and he spoke words to her which broke through the grief, and held out such promise on the other side of death: 'Woman, here is your son.' And to John, 'Here is your mother.' Something happened in Mary's heart at the foot of the cross, as her own dear Son bore away the sins of the world. And something soon happened to turn that midnight to noonday, and light up the whole world with risen glory.

But we must not run ahead of ourselves, for it was today that Brother David died, and as I pray for him I commend him into the hands of the dying and risen Saviour. We have an 'Office of Commendation' for a brother or sister on their death, and you may like to share one of the prayers from it, substituting your loved ones' name/s where I have included *David*.

PRAYER

David, *our companion in faith and* brother *in Christ, we entrust you to God who created you.*

May you return to the Most High who formed you from the dust of the earth.

May the angels and the saints come to meet you as you go forth from this life.

May Christ, who was crucified for you, take you into his kingdom.

May Christ the Good Shepherd give you a place within his flock.

May Christ forgive you your sins and keep you among his people.

May you see your Redeemer face to face and delight in the vision of God for ever. Amen.

RESPONSE

Share today in the Church's liturgy for Good Friday, but if this is not possible, then spend some time before a cross or crucifix reading one of the accounts of the Passion of Christ.

You will find you need to be alone for some part of the day, so arrange beforehand with a friend or relative to care for children or other responsibilities for an hour or two.

Do not be afraid of solitude, sorrow and meditation on the dying of Jesus on this day. It is out of such times of meditation and confrontation with those deep truths that new life appears, and Good Friday is especially the appropriate day.

Holy Saturday

A New Tomb in the Hewn Rock

MATTHEW 27:57-66; 1 PETER 3:18-20

When it was evening, there came a rich man from Arimathea, named Joseph, who was also a disciple of Jesus. He went to Pilate and asked for the body of Jesus; then Pilate ordered it to be given to him. So Joseph took the body and wrapped it in a clean linen cloth, and laid it in his own new tomb, which he had hewn in the rock. He then rolled a great stone to the door of the tomb and went away.

Christ also suffered for sins once for all, the righteous for the unrighteous, in order to bring you to God. He was put to death in the flesh, but made alive in the Spirit, in which also he went and made a proclamation to the spirits in prison. . . .

I held my breath when I first gazed at Michaelangelo's *Pieta* in St Peter's Church, Rome. There was Mary, sculpted in white marble, holding her dead Son in her arms — breathtakingly beautiful. Part of the reason why I held my breath was because a little while before, a man had attacked the sculpture with a hammer!

It is like that today. I cannot conceive of anyone wanting to desecrate this day — to shout, to feast, to make merry. A kind of passivity holds me — a stillness and quietness that is appropriate, because the Beloved is laid in the tomb and there is a sense of waiting in the air. Joseph of Arimathea, the secret disciple but now courageous and bold, begged the body of Jesus from Pilate, tenderly anointed and wrapped it in linen, and laid it in his own prepared tomb hewn in the rock. Waiting. So today I find myself physically slowing down, mentally concentrated, and spiritually feeling the importance of not wanting to give counsel, interfere in anyone else's affairs, or beat upon heaven's door with my incessant questions, petitions or intercessions — this is not the day for it.

But I also have a sense that beneath the surface, in the secret places, in the hidden counsels of God, something else is happening. The clue is given in those verses from the First Epistle of Peter. They say that Jesus, having been put to death in the flesh but alive in the Spirit, went to the prison house of Hades and sounded a mighty proclamation to the imprisoned spirits of former times. If this is linked to the descending and ascending Christ in Ephesians 4:6-10, the substance of that proclamation is freedom from the prison and gifts from the risen Christ to the prisoners.

This mythological picture is expressed beautifully in some of the resurrection icons of the eastern Church, so different from the western depictions of Christ rising alone. The icons reveal Christ harrowing hell, mightily treading down hell's bronze doors, breaking the chains, fetters and locks, raising Adam, Eve, the patriarchs and all the sighing, yearning prisoners of Hades, into the glory of his risen life.

So I am aware in my own life that as I feel this passivity, restfulness, waiting, and even a certain melancholy in the entombment of the body of Jesus, something else is going on. In the deep and secret places of my psyche, in the secret counsels of God, for my good there is a stirring of the divine Life, and I know that 'all shall be well'. It gives me immense joy today to know that the kingdom is bigger than the Church, that 'as all die in Adam, so all will be made alive in Christ . . . that God may be all in all.' (1 Corinthians 15:20-28) I cannot begin to understand the measure of such love, of such a divine embrace, but I wait today, with bated breath – for something is about to happen.

PRAYER

Lord Jesus, harrower of hell:
There is no depth of sorrow or darkness that you have not
  penetrated, no dark prison from which you can be
  excluded.
Descend today into the prison-houses of our world and
  proclaim forgiveness, deliverance and healing to the poor
  captives of body, mind and spirit.
In the silent waiting of my own heart, let the flicker of new
  hope burn steadily into the flame of life and love;
Lead me into and beyond the darkness of death, until the
  dawning glory of eternity. Amen.

RESPONSE

You are meant to be quiet today, and not go rushing around organizing your own or other's lives. Kneel or sit quietly in your worship place and let your meditation be guided by

today's reflection, using the following hymn for Holy Saturday.
If you can find an icon on the theme, then include it in your
meditation.

CHRIST HARROWS HELL

Now while the body, quiet and still
Lies wrapped in bands of linen fair,
The glow of life and warmth and power
Flickers in hell's cold, darkling air.

And while the myrrh and aloes' balm
Perfume his feet and hands and head,
Christ's spreading light pierces the gloom
And lights the kingdom of the dead.

The doors of bronze burst at his cry,
And all the sons of Adam wake,
He harrows hell and breaks death's bonds,
And all the powers of darkness shake.

Adam and Eve, that primal pair
Are led on high to liberty,
While patriarch and prophet stand
And sing the song of jubilee.

The dying thief beholds his Lord,
Fulfilled the promise of the King,
While saints of that first covenant
Join with angelic choirs and sing.

The breaking of the Easter dawn
Reveals the body of the Lord
Endued with life and love and power,
Incarnate is the Eternal Word!

All glory, Christ, our risen King,
Who with the Father reigns above
Within the Holy Spirit's bond,
Eternal life and light and love. Amen.

EASTER DAY
Let the Alleluias Begin!

He is not here he is risen

Easter Day

Let the Alleluias Begin!

JOHN 20:1-18

*J*esus said to her, 'Woman, why are you weeping? Whom are you looking for?'

Supposing him to be the gardener, she said to him, 'Sir, if you have carried him away, tell me where you have laid him, and I will take him away.'

Jesus said to her, 'Mary!' She turned and said to him in Hebrew, 'Rabbouni!; (which means Teacher). Jesus said to her, 'Do not hold on to me, because I have not yet ascended to the Father. But go to my brothers and say to them, "I am ascending to my Father and your Father, to my God and your God."'

This is the most wonderful day of the year – the Alleluias can begin again because after the sad story of betrayal, treachery, suffering, pain and death the breath of God has swept through the garden sepulchre, and the Lord is risen. Alleluia!

There are two aspects to our reading today. First, the empty tomb, and then the appearance of the risen Lord. The tomb story is exciting drama, and though the fact of the tomb being empty is negative evidence, yet the eye of faith saw what was clearly implied (v 8).

Mary Magdalene, after the devastation of seeing the broken seal and the stone moved from the tomb in the dark grey morning, ran to Peter and John, thinking that Jesus' body had been removed by the authorities or had been robbed. Peter was there – what courage he must have had to return to the other disciples after his denial, and John the beloved disciple. They upped and ran immediately. John, being younger, outran Peter, and arriving, looked in. Peter soon came behind breathlessly, and entered the tomb.

The sight that met them is made clear by the evangelist. The grave-clothes were not missing, were not dishevelled or even folded, but still in their original folds – the Greek says just that. What did it mean? John saw, understood, believed. The body had dematerialized in its transformation from a mortal to an immortal, spiritual body. So there was continuity in that the crucified body had been taken up into the body of glory, and there was discontinuity in that it was no longer mortal or crudely material.

Crown him, the Lord of love;
Behold his hands and side,
Those wounds, yet visible above
In beauty glorified.

This is the proto-type of Paul's teaching in 1 Corinthians 15:20, 42-50, and is what was believed, witnessed and taught in the early Church. The empty tomb may be negative evidence, but its witness in what had happened is vital and wonderful.

Now the appearance. Mary returned after Peter and John

had left the garden. She could not keep away, and it is significant that the first person to whom our Lord appeared was a woman, and a woman who had experienced his saving, healing power – she loved much!

She is important to us today, for first of all she looked for the wrong thing in the wrong place. She sought a dead Christ and faced the tomb. There are so many who revere, honour and even follow the Christ 'who used to be'. The post-Easter experience is *radically* different, in that Jesus is alive – personal and communal relationship is offered today – we do not honour his memory but rejoice in his risen life.

Then when he sought her in her tears, she did not perceive him, though she saw him, and it was not simply her tears that blinded her, but her lack of expectation. If we approach the texts with preconceived unbelief and prejudice we shall not perceive him either, for the paradoxes and confusion in the texts indicate the truth and vitality of the reality of the risen Christ. Jesus gazed into her soul, spoke the personal, saving word, 'Mary!' and there is immediate and ecstatic recognition which has to be restrained in its expression.

Well here it is – here *he* is today – confronting Mary Magdalene while the exciting implications of the empty tomb are being spread by Peter and John among the disciples. And here he is, before you and me in the secret quietness of our sharing together. He is here! He is risen! Let the Alleluias begin!

PRAYER

Lord Jesus, risen and glorified:
I have followed your footsteps through the days of Lent,
tracing the beauty of your teaching, the compassion of
your miracles, the tenderness of your dealing with sinners;
I have walked the path of your grief and pain, your bearing
of the load of our sins and sorrows at Calvary, until my
heart has been bowed in shame and tears.
Then, in the quietness and darkness of these last few days,
the flickering light of hope has burned within, and this
morning I was awakened with the new song of Easter
ringing in my heart, and you are risen from the dead!
Because of all these wonderful happenings, I would yield
myself to you, asking that your risen life may transform
me within the fellowship of your Church. Inflame our
hearts so that your risen life may light the path of so
many in our world who continue to walk in darkness.
Amen.

RESPONSE

The response of the early Church to the risen Lord was one of looking to the Holy Spirit for power and holiness, witness and proclamation of the Gospel of Christ in its fullness, and an experiential radiance which drew others into the believing fellowship. After listening to the Gospel reading at today's eucharist, and sharing joyful worship with fellow-believers, wander out into fields, parkland or even a garden, and spend fifteen minutes reflecting on the Holy Spirit's manifestation of resurrection life in the buds, blossoms and flowers or springtime – and add your praises to theirs.

Groups

Share together the main thrust of your Lenten pilgrimage, and ask what new awareness and possibilities have opened up for you as a result of this journey.

Then sit together in a circle, linking hands and praying especially for the sister or brother on your right and left, while they pray for you.

Then let the Alleluias begin!